T0161900

The Marvelous Millennial's Manual
To Modern Manners

ADVANCE PRAISE FOR *The Marvelous Millennial's Manual to Modern Manners*

"Good manners and etiquette in our daily lives will never go out style. Thanks to Catherine and Jessica's terrific book we are reminded that living by The Golden Rule of treating others the way you would like to be treated is a fundamental skill that should be a part of our daily lives with every single human interaction we have. As they rightly state, possessing good manners means you also possess a certain 'kindness of spirit'. What a valuable lesson for millennials in this fast-paced, rapidly changing technological world. As a parent, I commend the authors for helping our nation's young people understand that a solid foundation of manners, social skills, and business etiquette training can help make their careers more fulfilling, their goals more attainable, and their lives more pleasant."

ANITA MCBRIDE, Executive in Residence, School of Public Affairs at American University and the former Assistant to President George W. Bush and Chief of Staff to the First Lady Laura Bush from 2005-2009.

"Jessica and Catherine's advice is valuable because they express themselves every day with the modern manners they write about. This book isn't just about their advice, it's how they live their lives. I know because I have had the privilege of working with them and viewing them 'in action.' Their manners translate to real-life kindness and consideration of others. Read the book and make your life easier and more pleasant every day!"

AMY SHOWALTER, Author, *The Underdog Edge*, The Showalter Group, Inc.

"Jessica Marventano and Catherine Wallace have written a book that is the perfect antidote to the toxic culture that we too often see in today's America. They remind us of the power of being kind, of giving people the benefit of the doubt, and of knowing the rules so that you can be comfortable in any room you walk into. Buy this for every millennial you know, but make sure to read it yourself—there is a lot in here that I didn't know but wish I had learned years ago!"

SUSANNAH WELLFORD, President & Founder, Running Start, an organization designed to raise the political voice of young women in America.

"Every truly successful person I know—especially those with whom others want to work—understands the importance of good manners and the value of thoughtfulness, small gestures, and kindness. As a corporate and non-profit board director, former executive at PwC, and the creator of the "She Said/She Said" podcast, I see these small gestures play out in big ways every single day. Thank you to *The Marvelous Millennial's Manual for Modern Manners* for dusting off and modernizing the timeless value of etiquette in the workplace and society."

LAURA COX KAPLAN, Creator & Host at She Said/She Said Podcast: Insight. Inspiration. Impact. Former Principal-in-Charge of U.S. Government, Regulatory Affairs & Public Policy at PricewaterhouseCoopers, LLP

"If you listed 10 characteristics of human behavior that underpin a civil society, knowing where the dessert fork goes in a table setting might not be one of them. But good manners, proper etiquette and kindness are far more important to our human interrelationships than you think, particularly when they are exercised in business, political, social and, yes, personal relationships. The erosion of civil behavior—

the effort to listen to one another and the simple lack of manners—has had a profoundly negative impact on our lives and society as a whole. Thankfully, this new book, *The Marvelous Millennial's Manual to Modern Manners*, offers an informative and entertaining re-introduction to, and hopefully revival of, the importance of manners and etiquette and how each should be practiced in all kinds of settings. It is a must read for the millennial generation to whom the book is directed. Please read it and thank you for doing so."

THALIA ASSURAS, President, Assuras Communications LLC and formerly an anchor and correspondent at ABC and CBS networks.

The Marvelous Millennial's Manual

MODERN MANNERS

*Professional Success
and Happiness with the
Help of Business Etiquette*

JESSICA W. MARVENTANO
CATHERINE CRANE WALLACE

NEW YORK

LONDON • NASHVILLE • MELBOURNE • VANCOUVER

The Marvelous Millennial's Manual To Modern Manners

Professional Success and Happiness with the Help of Business Etiquette

Published in New York, New York, by Morgan James Publishing. Morgan James is a trademark of Morgan James, LLC. www.MorganJamesPublishing.com

ISBN 9781642790535 paperback
ISBN 9781642790542 eBook
Library of Congress Control Number: 2018940847

Cover Design by:
Rachel Lopez
www.r2cdesign.com

Interior Design by:
Chris Treccani
www.3dogcreative.net

Illustrations by:
Wendy Sefcik

Morgan James is a proud partner of Habitat for Humanity Peninsula and Greater Williamsburg. Partners in building since 2006.

Get involved today! Visit
MorganJamesPublishing.com/giving-back

"To our family, we love hard."

TABLE OF CONTENTS

ACKNOWLEDGMENTS

We are especially grateful to those who helped us out on the fun adventure of Marvelously Well-Mannered. First and foremost, we are thankful for the love and support of our family. Jennifer Montesano's sound judgement, attention to detail, good nature, and enthusiasm helped bring shape to many of our ideas. Isabella, Olivia, and Catherine are the three lovely ladies who inspired our board game, Kindness Kingdom. Craig Montesano has a keen eye to both the spoken and written word. Thank you for sharing. David Marventano, your unwavering patience and support made this all possible.

We have a great squad of ladies. Diane Warren was one of our earliest cheerleaders with a great head for business! Wendy Sefcik of Broxen Box Designs helped turn our vision into beautiful illustrations in the book and colorful and fanciful artwork on the Kindness Kingdom game board. Thalia Assuras helped us navigate the talk show circuit and spread the word that manners do matter. Sara Morris was a great sounding board, occasional fill-in in the IT department, and just there to help with whatever we needed. She now enthusiastically talks about passing bread baskets. Amy Showalter's willingness to share what she knows and help make connections is truly amazing. Gena Zak, the lovely lady extraordinaire of the Capitol Hill Club, has worked with us over the years to provide a whole host of educational and engaging etiquette classes. This collaboration has meant the world to us, thank you!

Thank you to the fantastic team at Morgan James Publishing for helping us at every step along the way, especially, Terry Whalin, Tiffany Gibson and Aubrey Kosa.

We would be remiss if we didn't mention Esther Reilly Crane, Catherine's mum who started her down the proper, polite path. Her kindness and words of wisdom are in this book. Last, but not least, our gratitude goes to Mary Wallace, Jessica's paternal grandmother who gifted Jessica with her very first etiquette book. Jessica poured over that 1882 social cyclopedia on every visit. Mary had it rebound, and it sits on our library shelf today. How marvelous!

INTRODUCTION

Take Heart, It's Not You!

The millennial generation–those born between 1982 and 2004[1]–has so much positive to offer[2]. You have empathy, open-mindedness, a heartfelt connection to others, fierce optimism, and the technological promise that comes with being our country's first Digital Native generation[3]. Indeed, your social-connectedness has helped us all embrace the wonder of the Internet and make digital technology an everyday tool. For the older generations, digital technology is a learned skill, but for millennials, it is a cognitive skill. Just ask any parent who has had to ask someone younger to help them post a picture, remotely log in to their work intranet, or download an app.

And just like the generations that came before millennials, society will take the good you bring to the table and leave behind the bad. Earlier generations have introduced to society new styles of music, new styles of art, new advances in technology. And the best of the best remains. So too will the millennial generation make its mark. But the road won't be easy. Just like those earlier generations, yours will first get blamed for society's ills before the good you bring to the table is acknowledged[4].

The children now love luxury; they have bad manners, contempt for authority; they show disrespect for elders and love chatter in place of exercise. Children are now tyrants, not the servants of their households. They no longer rise when elders enter the room. They contradict their parents, chatter before company, gobble up dainties at the table, cross their legs, and tyrannize their teachers.

That quote is most often attributed to Socrates who lived during the fourth century BC[5]. Older generations have placed the blame for society's ills on younger generations since time began. Parents thought the "Baby Boom" generation was going to hell in a handbasket because of Elvis Presley hip-swiveling. Take heart in knowing that blaming the younger generation for the ills of present day society is nothing new.

It's not you and your generation after all.

Truthfully, your generation has wonderful attributes that should be celebrated. What most of the millennial generation doesn't have, however, is a solid foundation of manners, social skills, and business etiquette training that can help make your careers more fulfilling, your goals more attainable, and your lives more pleasant. These skills are learned skills; they are not cognitive skills. It will take some time and effort on your part to master them.

If anyone is to be blamed for this lack of skill development it's–bless their hearts–your loving, omnipresent, helicopter parents. Parents who had the best intentions telling you that you could be anything you wanted to be and who tried to make you happier and make everything easier and safer. But in this type of parenting approach some very important things were lost a bit–the focus on consistent hard work, the encouragement of developing grit (you don't get a trophy just for showing up), and imparting the lesson of the vital importance of manners, that you shouldn't just think of yourself to the exclusion of others. Those are the foundational elements of self-respect, a necessary characteristic for also having respect for others and for a functioning, civilized society. While you as a generation didn't create this skill deficit problem, it is up to you to help solve that problem.

And we are going to help you take it from here.

Since 2015, the millennial generation has been the largest segment of the US business population (then 35 percent)[6], working alongside two generations of professional colleagues, each with their own ideas of what is appropriate or not in the work setting. Add to this the ubiquitous presence of technology in lieu of face-to-face interactions, open work space floor plans instead of your own space, and the Friday casual dress code and mindset seeping into the other days of the week and you have a caustic incivility cocktail. The garnish is the fact that while people in large part don't intend to be rude, they sometimes end up being rude simply because they aren't self-aware. They don't think about how their actions impact other people or even realize that their actions influence what others think of them. Unsurprisingly, many of you may be experiencing frustration in these early years of your professional career as a result of those very things.

We joyfully wrote this book to teach the rules of business etiquette and equip millennials (and perhaps even other generations) with manners, social skills, and dining skills–everything you need to put your best polite and polished foot forward in your professional life. These skills are your tools for success–professionally and personally. Society needs the millennial generation to succeed. Why? Because by 2025, your generation will make up 75 percent of America's workforce[7]. You will soon be writing the rules for corporate America and we want you to get it right.

We are on your team!

Nice is Best

Possessing both good manners and a working knowledge of the rules of etiquette makes life easier, pure and simple. You are more comfortable in all situations of everyday life both personal and professional–it makes no difference where you are–and you will always be at ease because you are confident in your own skin. You won't need to spend time worrying about your own presentation because you know what you want your personal brand to be and how to act accordingly. In turn, you will be able to afford to take the time to make others around you feel welcomed and at ease. When you are able to do that, others want to be around you and work with you. Every occasion becomes more enjoyable.

How marvelous does that sound?

Possessing good manners means you also possess a certain "kindness of spirit"–a *je ne sais quoi*–that enables you to be considerate of other people, charm them, and make them feel wanted, welcome, and respected. You follow The Golden Rule of treating others the way you would like to be treated, but you also take care to go one step further. We like to call this extra step The Platinum Rule. The Platinum Rule is that you appreciate that everyone is an individual with their own quirks and eccentricities and you exercise restraint and compassion so as not to purposefully bother others more sensitive than yourself. You know there is no need to needle others or treat every conversation like a debate. Moreover, you don't go out of your way to be offended by others. You assume the best in others and generously give the benefit of the doubt and forgive transgressions because when someone acts rudely you know it says much more about them than you.

Etiquette, on the other hand, serves as a roadmap of civilized society and allows us to showcase that kindness of spirit, along with graciousness and marvelous manners, by taking the appropriate action at the appropriate time. When individuals know the rules of etiquette and have a certain *savoir vivre*–knowledge of the ways of polite society–and act accordingly, common cordiality and civility develop and, resultantly, actual and potential problems diminish. How marvelous. And how necessary.

Society, too, needs manners to properly function. Simply put, chaos ensues without the generous heart and kindness of spirit associated with manners and well-known rules of the road for polite society[8]. Misunderstandings, slights, and offenses can take on a life of their own, impeding productive and pleasant progress, not to mention leading to potentially dangerous situations. Manners ensure the proper well-being and safety of everyone.

As such an integral part of society, manners, social skills, and business etiquette are important tools for millennials to possess, especially as many jobs are becoming automated. The World Economic Forum's 2016 Future of Jobs Report estimates that by 2020, over 5 million jobs will be lost to automation.

Now, instead of panicking, let's focus. Where will future jobs come from? (And we firmly believe there still will be jobs–as opposed to universal basic income courtesy of the federal government. People want to work. People need jobs and a purpose in order to have dignity and self-respect.)

Unsurprisingly, job growth will be in areas where human social skills are needed–areas where computers simply cannot replicate the human ability of being in the moment, socially savvy, and emotionally intelligent[9]. Unfortunately, today many employers say these critical skills are in short supply, with one employer going so far as to put "common sense" on a sign describing the skills they were looking for in a new hire[10]. Employers are desperate for employees with the ability to communicate, work with other people in a team environment, be on time, think critically and creatively to find solutions, and be socially savvy. These are not skills yet associated with computers–which is good news for us!

Even more good news? Manners, business etiquette, and social skills are all skills that you can learn! And you should want to learn these skills because studies show that a whopping 85 percent of one's professional success is connected to one's people skills[11]. Manners, the rules of etiquette, and social skills are the very foundation of good people skills. Can you even have good people skills if you don't know how to treat someone? Having this critical skill set will make you happier and more successful–and everyone who encounters you too. And in business–as in life–you rarely succeed on your own. We need other people, a community.

The great thing about manners is that kindness begets kindness. When someone is nice to you, aren't you likely to be nice back? And to the next person you encounter? Of course you are.

Corporate America is starting to pay attention. Businesses do care if their workplace–and those working in it–is civil because good manners are good for the bottom line. Conversely, incivility is bad for business. Not only does it cause companies to lose customers, but incivility keeps companies from attracting and retaining top-drawer staff. It distracts employees from their actual work as they spend time worrying about (and trying to avoid) toxic colleagues[12]. And good people eventually leave jobs because of incivility[13]. Just as kindness begets kindness, unfortunately the opposite is also true. Rudeness is contagious[14]. One study found that when nice employees are subjected to repeated rude behavior, 47 percent of them will become rude as they lose the self-control necessary to stay calm and not respond with retaliatory rudeness themselves[15]. In the study, employees were bombarded with three rude emails a day for 70 days. The rude behavior literally wore them down. As the saying goes, one bad apple can spoil the whole bunch.

Learning the rules of etiquette and how to be well-mannered takes time and consistency if they are truly to become engrained in someone. And that is what we want–for the skills to be engrained in each one of us, not taken out and dusted off and used only "as needed". Manners are always needed.

Manners are the happy way of doing things; each one a stroke of genius or of love, now repeated and hardened into usage. – RALPH WALDO EMERSON

Manners, social skills, and business etiquette skills are not something we save for special occasions or the VIPs. These skills should be showcased every single work day with every single human interaction we have.

This book can be viewed as your private coach, your manners mentor, if you will, that teaches you what to do and how to do it, so that you can learn, grow, succeed, and be happy.

We certainly aren't striving for perfection here. Everyone–and we mean everyone, us included–commits etiquette faux pas. What we are after is to get you into the mindset of waking up every day trying your best to be well-mannered and knowing that when you fall short (again, we all do), all is not lost because you can start anew tomorrow. There is an endless supply of manners in each of us waiting to be shared with everyone we encounter. The following sections will provide you with the most up-to-date and relevant personal branding, business etiquette, and dining skills information.

Remember, there is **no** downside to being well-mannered.

PART I

BRANDING.

Put Your Best, Polite, Polished Foot Forward

Every behavior is associated with your brand. It is important to intentionally create and maintain a personal brand if you want positive words associated with you. "She's a team player." "He goes the extra mile." "She is reliable." Once you have a negative word associated with you, it takes time and effort to overcome it. You never want someone to say, "She is difficult to work with." "He never meets deadlines." "You have to walk on eggshells around him." It takes five seconds for someone to form a first impression of you. Let them form the impression that will help lead to your success.

Making a Good First Impression

You have five seconds. Yes, just five seconds. That's it. All you have to make a first impression.

First impressions are lasting, in life and in business. It's true that you can sometimes change someone's first impression of you, but it takes time–a lot of time, patience, and consistency in your rebranding. That is why it's best to think about what you want people to think of you (and not think of you) and then *intentionally* act accordingly from the get-go.

Of your first impression, an astounding 55 percent of the message your body sends is attributed to the way you look as well as the confidence you exude and your body language. Of the remaining, 38 percent of the message is from the way you speak, including the grammar you use and the tone you take. Only a paltry 7 **percent** of the message you send is based on the actual substance of your words. Without even realizing it, your body is constantly talking to the outside world.

What is yours saying?

Your *personal deportment* carries a lot of weight in the impression you make on others. What do we mean by personal deportment? Personal deportment refers to your manner of personal conduct and the way you behave, especially your physical bearing. There are two essential areas of personal deportment you should concentrate on in order to send confident signals to the rest of the world.

The first area of focus is your posture. Good posture means exactly what many of us were told growing up: stand up straight and proud. When you slouch, you are telling the world that you are self-conscious and don't want to be seen; you are drained and dreary. Basically, you are telling the world that you don't think you are worth it. Show some self-confidence by standing tall with your head held high. Imagine someone is gently pulling up a ribbon affixed to the top of your head. Your shoulders should be rolled down and back with your shoulder blades pulled closer together. It feels so good and is actually good for you physically when you stand this way–trust us! Standing straight means aligning your ears and shoulders with the shoulder blades pulled down and back. It makes you look slimmer and more confident and feel less stressed. In the back of our minds, we all know we should remember to stand straight, but it is becoming more and more of a challenge as we spend hours sitting behind our desks or hunched over our electronic devices.

Scarily, research shows that bending your head to read your electronic devices puts 60 pounds of pressure on your cervical spine (the part of the spine above the shoulders)[16]. So avoid the painful and unattractive "tech-neck" and put your phone down and look up. Engage and be present with your physical surroundings.

When you stand, try to evenly distribute your weight between your two feet. Rocking back and forth signals uncomfortableness. Let your arms fall loosely to your sides. Avoid tightly folding your arms across your chest because that makes you look unapproachable, unpleasant, and confrontational. Your movements should be purposeful, so don't fidget by touching your face, twirling your hair, or constantly pushing up your eye glasses (if your glasses move that much, get them adjusted).

Making eye contact when speaking instantly projects confidence and trustworthiness. Some people have a difficult time making eye contact. To help, try turning it into a game–enter every conversation by trying to figure out what eye color the other person has[17]. When you do that, you focus less on the fact that you are making eye contact and instead are more focused on trying to get an answer to the eye color question. Likewise, those who have difficulty making direct eye contact can focus on the small triangle described in the following paragraph, which makes you look like you are looking into their eyes when you actually aren't.

In a professional setting, you should always concentrate on the space between someone's eyebrows while talking to them (that small triangle referenced before). Imagine a dot there. That is the area of the face that means, "I am here to talk business." As you move down the face and chest, you go from a proper business gaze to a social gaze all the way to a more intimate one. It goes without saying, there is no reason to gaze at someone's chest (or other body parts). Keep all eyes up in business!

Eye contact signals to the other person that you are listening to them. It is hard to concentrate on what someone is saying when you are looking over their shoulder or elsewhere. When you focus on them, you look in control and pay more attention. This will help you become a better conversationalist.

In business, direct eye contact should be made between 40 and 60 percent of the time. Less than 40 percent and others think you are sneaky, shady, and insecure. *Why won't they look at me when talking about this important project? They must be hiding something or lying to me.* On the other hand, when you look at someone more than 60 percent of the time, the other person feels uncomfortable, thinking, *What is up with this freak staring at me? What do they want from me?*

Lastly, remember that when you look at someone, please smile. A smiling face shows kindness and confidence–a winning combination in any business setting. Smile, and the world smiles back.

Applying this in the real world

Q. If I am supposed to only make eye contact 40-60 percent of the time, where do I look the rest of the time?

A. The goal is to break up the eye contact so that it isn't so intense. You can look at the triangle spot between the eyes, you can look immediately to their side, you can look at others in the conversation group, you can look at a common object or reference material (a document, for example), or simply just around. But always come back to eye contact to show you are focused on the conversation at hand.

Q. When I am standing and talking in a business setting, I don't know what to do with my arms and hands. I feel awkward if I just let them hang down by my sides.

A. You want to appear as natural as possible. Standing completely still with arms frozen at your side is not being natural. Think in terms of avoiding fidgeting. In contrast, fluid, graceful movement is ok. If you are explaining something and want to animate a point using your hands, that is fine. We all do that. Envision yourself holding a ball between your two hands and your hands will be occupied in a way that doesn't look like nervous fidgeting.

Personal Deportment:

Grooming, Attitude, and Image

ike it or not, people tend to judge a book by its cover. And let's face it, without good personal hygiene, you don't have much. It is important to take pride in your appearance. It shows respect for yourself and for others whose paths you cross.

We assume you know the basics, namely that it is important to regularly bath, wash, comb and style your hair, use deodorant, and brush your teeth. These are the foundational steps of good grooming and are essential when you are working daily with others.

Bad breath is the kiss of death. People simply won't enjoy being around you. It is hard to know when your own breath is less than pleasant, but take note if people turn their head when you talk or take a step back to increase the space between you. The best things to do to guard against this are to regularly brush and floss your teeth, keep mints on hand, and keep hydrated. Mints are preferable to gum because chewing gum is not an attractive look. Some of us look like a cow chewing its cud. When you don't drink enough fluids, you don't produce saliva. Saliva is what helps keep your mouth clean and fresh by washing away odor-causing bacteria. Store a toothbrush and toothpaste at work to use after your morning coffee or lunch and before you head out for a meeting with clients.

Remember to **maintain your manicure**–by this we mean take care of your hands, men included! Nails should be filed, and cuticles should be smooth. Cream your hands and cuticles to prevent dry, rough hands and cracked cuticles. This will make it easier to refrain from picking at your fingers and nails. Overly decorative nails are not appropriate in most professional business settings, so use good judgment there. Women also sometimes overlook keeping their rings clean.

And let's not forget the feet. If your office allows open-toed shoes or sling-backs, maintain your feet–nails, polish, and heels. Men, if you are wearing sandals, maintain your feet as well.

Ladies should use **makeup** to enhance their look, not mask it. Likewise, too little makeup is as bad as too much makeup. When properly applied, makeup helps you look polished and fresh and, according to a study, more likable and competent[18]. Visit a nearby makeup counter to help you identify your proper makeup color palette and teach you application techniques. Also, there are countless YouTube videos on makeup application that can help get you started on a budget.

Personal upkeep is just that–**personal!** It is to be done in private. Do not clip, file or paint nails, brush or spray your hair, floss teeth, use toothpicks, or apply makeup in public–lipstick included. When you need to do some personal upkeep, simply excuse yourself and go to the powder room when you are out in public or otherwise on the go.

Go easy on the fragrance. Light perfume or men's cologne is appealing. Do not bath yourself in fragrance–your fragrance should not arrive before you do. It should only have a supporting role in your image. Be mindful that others may have allergies or sensitivities. You don't want your perfume to make those that work near you miserable. Be kind. If you aren't sure if you are using too much, ask a trusted and honest friend to assess your application.

Facial hair. Men, it should be neat. Don't come in unshaven. Mind you, there is a *huge* difference between unshaven and scruffy and maintaining deliberate facial hair. Don't look like you just rolled out of bed.

Just as our physical appearance impacts our interaction with others, so does our attitude. A **positive attitude** is priceless. People will enjoy being around you when you have a good attitude. Don't be a Debbi-Downer or chronic complainer. Don't complain, gossip, tease, or be mean to others. Instead, consciously try to cultivate a happy disposition, give others the benefit of the doubt, and have a good sense of humor. You are happy to be there and are ready to go.

The image you project should be one of confidence and self-respect. If you don't like yourself, it is hard for others to like you too. But don't go overboard and merge into arrogance.

"It's far more impressive when others discover your good qualities without your help." – MISS MANNERS

Self-confidence is a wonderful attribute. Most people need more of it. But some have been blessed with too much of a good thing when it morphs into boastful, entitled, self-centered behavior. People who act that way are a big bore. Don't you agree? Strive for a self-confident, grateful, and kind attitude. Truly self-confident people are kind to others because they don't have to tear anyone else down to make themselves feel better. You will be much more enjoyable to be around and work with if you are confident and comfortable with who you are.

Taken together, all of those personal deportment practices help you project the positive image necessary for a good personal brand.

Applying this in the real world.

Q. A colleague of mine goes overboard on the perfume. What can I do? My head aches every day from the fragrance.

A. Your situation is exactly why it is so important for people to be aware of how much fragrance they use. You don't want it to precede you. You don't want it to overwhelm your colleagues. If you are friends with your colleague, the most direct route is to talk to them in private and let them know that you are sensitive to their fragrance and it is causing headaches. Politely ask them to either lighten up or go without. If you are uncomfortable doing this, or don't think they would respond well to your direct request, talk to your manager or HR so they can rectify the situation. They might have more options available, such as switching office or desk assignments.

Q. How do I gain self-confidence without being arrogant?

A. Self-confidence is knowing–truly knowing–that you are worthy of the kindness, patience, and positive energy you should be giving others. Treating yourself well is the first step to gaining self-confidence. It does not mean that you think you are better than anyone else. It just means that you are worthy too. Every morning, remind yourself of things you like about yourself and things you do well–always focus on the positive.

Dress for Success

"The way we dress affects the way we think, the way we feel, the way we act, and the way others react to us."
– JUDITH RASBAND

As part of your outward appearance, your wardrobe reveals a lot about you. You want your wardrobe to accurately represent your "style". In the workplace, success should be part of your style. Taste should be part of your style. What is taste? According to Professor P.M. Forni, founder of the Johns Hopkins University Civility Project, "Someone with good taste is a member of an elite whose talent is choosing well."[19]

The image you project sets the tone for your business success. Your wardrobe works together with your personal deportment to create an image for the world to see, including your boss (and future boss), your colleagues, your customers, your clients, and industry peers.

What do you want to say with your appearance?

The goal of your work wardrobe should be to dress with taste and class so that your appearance works for you, not against you, in terms of advancing your career. Your appearance should be such that it helps you develop your career. It should never damage your career. You're in charge of the message your appearance sends. Remember, "clothes make the man–and the woman."

Everyone is different. You need to dress appropriately—so that your wardrobe is suitable for your body, your age[20], the occasion, the workplace (is it a conservative private equity firm or an edgy tech start-up?), the weather, and your wallet. Lastly, but of equal importance, is the need to add some signature flair that is a style all your own.

We view an outfit as a neat, clean, pressed suit of armor that can increase your confidence[21]. When you wear something made of a quality fabric in a flattering color, with the proper cut and fit, that is just right for the occasion, your workplace, and the weather, and is something that you can afford, and that you love, you feel good. You know you look good. And it takes your game up a notch. You genuinely feel better about your presentation when you know you look good.

When you dress with taste, your clothes are no longer a career liability. You aren't insecure or full of doubt about your appearance. Instead, your clothes are the icing on the cake by reinforcing your image of success. They are a positive for you, not a negative. They improve your career. They don't impede it.

Some people like to choose a palate of three to four colors and only buy pieces in that palate. Others like to wear the rainbow. Most of us are somewhere in between. Whatever your approach, learn what colors and cuts flatter you and don't deviate from them.

"Don't pay to look ugly" is Catherine's solid advice when it comes to fads. Don't follow a fad that doesn't work for you—no matter how much you adore it.

Befriend your local tailor and shoe cobbler. They will help extend the life of your wardrobe pieces, saving you time and money and making you look like a million bucks.

Dressing for the occasion is important if you don't want to get noticed for all the wrong reasons. When you don't properly dress for an occasion, it can cause others to question your judgment and abilities in general.

Find out what type of dress an event calls for–is it a business meeting in a conservative industry? If so, then an outfit with a pop of color or something small (pin, scarf, necklace for the ladies and socks or ties or pocket squares for the men) to highlight your personality will do. Is it a business meeting in a creative industry? If so, there is a little more leeway. Look to your organization's leadership for what is considered appropriate.

Many of us attend conferences that call for the "business casual" look. If that is the case, smart and crisp separates are key. In business-casual situations, follow the rule of three: put on a third item to look more pulled together. For women, the third piece can be a scarf, a jacket, a wrap, a sweater, etc., while for men, a blazer or sweater would be the more obvious choice.

Learn to decode dress codes of the events you attend. Hopefully, your host will let you know what is expected. When in doubt, it's okay to ask the host or dress one level up from what you think is appropriate. In general, it is better to overdress than underdress. Here are the most common dress codes and what they mean:

- Black-Tie: Note, this dress style is properly reserved for 6:00 PM or after. Tuxedos for men. Fancy cocktail or long evening gowns with evening shoes and accessories for women.
- Cocktail: Dark suit and tie for men. Fancy, tea-length or knee-length cocktail dresses or dressy separates for women.

If going straight to an event from work, dress up your suit or work dress with jewelry, an evening clutch, and dress shoes (not a work pump).

- Business: Suit, tie, and dressy leather shoes for men, dress or suit and heels for women.
- Business Casual/Dressy Casual: This means different things at different companies. Take cues from your leadership, but in general: Sports coat/blazer, collared shirts, kakis or slacks or dark jeans and no tie for men. Professional separates for women (pants (including dark jeans if appropriate for your environment)/skirt or dresses with sweaters or jackets), adding a third clothing element as described previously. More casual shoes, including flats for women. If sneakers are appropriate in your office, keep them neat and clean.
- Casual: Clean, neat, and crisp separates that men and women can wear to BBQ, sporting events, or casual get-togethers with friends. Plain t-shirts, sandals, and sneakers are permissible.
- Resort Casual: For both men and women, clothing that is suitable for a pool-side event.
- Holiday Festive: This is an invitation for both men and women to add color, sparkle, and festiveness into your clothing and accessories.

Remember that in most work places, business casual does not mean weekend casual, sweats, or athletic lounge-wear. If you aren't sure what dress code an event calls for, try to find out what others who are also attending will be wearing or if you feel comfortable, ask the host or organizer of the event.

Whatever the occasion, we like to try to dress a step above what is called for–to "dress like the host", so to speak. By putting a touch more effort into your outfit, you will create a confident and tasteful presentation. (Note, this does not mean jumping to black-tie when an event is not identified as such.)

Of course, as young professionals the question is how to afford quality articles of clothing to build out your professional wardrobe. You *can* dress with taste, no matter what your budget. Certainly do not overspend, but whatever you can afford to buy, make sure you properly care for it. Shine and re-heel your shoes. Mend a hem. Reinforce a loose button. Iron or steam your clothes. Wash clothes according to their directions. Don't ever wear soiled, wrinkled, or worn clothes, especially in the workplace. **Sloppy is not a look of success**.

Yes, many tech CEOs wear t-shirts and sweatshirts. When you are the CEO, you can set the tone. Until then, dress to impress in your organization.

Don't forget your accessories. Keep purses, shoes, scarves, umbrellas, backpacks, work bags, and the like in top form. They should complement your look, not complicate it.

> *"Shabby shoes with a worn heel are as obvious as a missing button but not as easily forgiven."* – ESTHER CRANE

People will forgive a missing button, assuming you just lost it. But worn heels, scuffed shoes, a beat-up purse send the signal that you are sloppy with their sad states. That is not a nice message to send. Neither is it a kind look.

And remember, *"you aren't dressed without a smile."* - from the movie *Annie*

> *"Nothing succeeds like the appearance of success."*
> – CHRISTOPHER LASCH

Applying this in the real world

Q. I am most productive when I am most comfortable. Why can't I wear my sweats to the office when I am not seeing clients?

A. Unless it is against your company policy, you can. But the real question is: should you? The answer depends on how your organization's leadership dresses, what they think of your type of dress, and if you want to get ahead in that organization. If they don't dress like that and you aspire to move up the corporate ladder, you should probably refrain from dressing that way. You want to dress in a way that signals to your boss and your peers that you are a "professional" in your field. By not dressing that way in front of clients, you already are conceding that your sweats are not a professional look.

Q. I like how I look in tight, short dresses and feel most confident in them. Confidence is important at work, so can I dress in a way that makes me feel most confident and self-assured?

A. Self-confidence is an important key ingredient to business success. The question to answer is if your style of dress is appropriate for your workplace. We would suggest it isn't appropriate if it distracts others from recognizing your skills and contributions at work or your peers and higher-ups don't take you seriously. If your choice of wardrobe is what people notice most about you to the point that it eclipses the great work you do, then you need to decide if your wardrobe is working for you or against you. You need not dress primly without any personality. You just need to dress appropriately so that you don't become a roadblock to your own success.

Making Time for Manners

"Manners require time, and nothing is more vulgar than haste."
– Ralph Waldo Emerson

Honking your horn on the way to work. Not holding the elevator for the person trying to catch the doors but frantically pushing the "close" button instead. Being short and obnoxious with the new barista at your regular coffee shop. Acting visibly exasperated at an older patron slowly counting money or asking questions of the sales clerk before you in line. Snapping at your children, your siblings, your assistant or your parents to "hurry up". Why do people do these things? Is everyone just rude?

We don't think most people wake up intending to be rude. Rather, they are usually just running late and trying to do too many things at once. Today, we try to cram more into every day, hour, and minute than previous generations. And millennials like to multi-task to get it all done. It can be very overwhelming.

Despite the overwhelm, we must reject the pattern of rudeness (especially our own) that seems to come with our faster-paced lives. One of the most impactful steps you can take to be consistently well-mannered is to learn to manage your time and not be late. Tardiness, after all, is a top etiquette faux pas itself.

Think about it. Aren't you more kind, patient, and forgiving when you have the "time" to be so?

It takes discipline and planning to wisely manage your time. When you do manage your time, the resultant dividends are marvelous. You are more organized, efficient, pleasant, and less flustered. You feel more in control. Life is more enjoyable for you and those who encounter you.

Being on time for all business affairs–breakfasts, lunches, dinners, receptions, weekly team meetings, appointments with clients–tells the other people with whom you are meeting that you respect them and value *their* time too. Conversely, rushing in breathlessly or texting "I'm on my way" does not reflect well on you. Just because you can reach them to let them know you are late (which is the least you can do) does not mean you are excused from learning to plan accordingly and be on time. I know of one executive who used to lock the conference room door because he was so irritated at team members waltzing in late, disrupting the meeting as they sought to get caught up on what they missed. It was clear to him that those employees didn't value his time (the boss) or their colleagues' time. Bad form.

If you want to be considered well-mannered, you need to learn to manage your time, so you don't waste anyone else's by being late. We advise against setting your clocks ahead–we don't know about you, but it just confuses us. You don't need to trick yourself. Just make the conscious decision that you will respect yours and others' time and act accordingly. Set yourself up for success in this area by trying these helpful tips.

Start your day off on the right foot by **preparing the night before**. Lay out your clothes, pack your bag, and put items you need to take with you to the office near your entrance. This will make sure your morning routine is less hectic. Then get up on time–don't hit snooze, just get up already. You want to avoid running late in the morning or you may be playing catch up for the rest of the day.

Tell yourself you are going to **arrive a few minutes early** to every appointment you have. Accurately plan for how long the commute is and add a buffer of fifteen minutes for unanticipated problems so you aren't arriving with no time to spare. Then use the spare few minutes once you arrive to do something for yourself. You can relax with a book, or listen to a podcast, check your social media accounts, or dash off a few notes. Or you can be productive and review material for your appointment or attend to some online chores (paying a bill, ordering something, or otherwise tackling an item on your "to-do" list). Soon you will look forward to and relish these few extra relaxing or productive minutes throughout the day. And they will add up to quality "me" time over the course of a week.

Just as you prepared to get out your front door early at the beginning of the workday, make sure you **schedule "prep" time** so you can get yourself ready and gather materials you need for every appointment throughout the day. Have everything ready to go so when you need to leave it is all right there waiting for you. The goal here is to avoid the last minute and often frantic search for files, shoes, keys, phones, etc.

Managing your time enables you to have time to be the thoughtful person you are meant to be. You will be considerate of other people, which is at the core of being well-mannered. That is a must for a polished and professional personal brand.

"Life be not so short but that there is always time for courtesy."
– RALPH WALDO EMERSON

Applying this in the real world

Q. I start off with the best of intentions every morning. But by mid-day I am behind on meetings and projects and end up keeping people waiting. What can I do?

A. Try scheduling some "15 minute catch-up" windows in your work day–one in the morning and one in the afternoon–to help you get back on track if any meetings run late or your schedule otherwise gets off track.

Q. I am good about being on time. But the people I meet with are always running late. That throws me off. What should I do?

A. You need to zealously guard your time. If an appointment or meeting starts late through no fault of your own and you can't make up the time on the back end, politely let the other person know that. Use your judgment if the other person running late is a client, potential client, or your boss. But to the extent you can, don't let others get you off track. If you know that a person you work with always runs late, take that into consideration as you plan your schedule.

5

Don't Be an Etiquette Buster

Are you an etiquette buster? Are you one of those people who say something dismissive when someone tries to make something a bit more special for you than is absolutely necessary? Miss Manners calls these people "etiquette busters" because they rain on others' parades and you are one if you say one of the following phrases in response to someone's act of kindness toward you: [22]

- "I can hold the door myself."
- "I can get my own chair."
- "I can carry my bags myself."
- "I am fine standing."
- "Please don't go to any fuss, it's just me!"
- "Plastic glasses are fine."
- "Don't bring out the crystal and china for me!"
- "Paper napkins and plastic forks work for me."
- "No need to be so fancy!"
- "You don't have to impress me!"
- "No problem."
- "It was nothing."

Next time you want to say one of these phrases in response to someone's niceness or hospitality, please don't. Instead, appreciate that someone wanted to treat you with respect by giving you a nicety–whether it is as simple as holding the door for you, offering you their seat, or helping you with your own seat at the dining table. With today's crisis in civility, do you really want to reject someone's attempt to be nice to you?

Likewise, when someone tries to make what could otherwise be an ordinary event a bit more special for you, say, "Thank you." You are worth it. This means, when your colleague invites you over for dinner, don't make them feel bad or foolish for using linen, real glasses, or decorating for the event.

It is also important to know that you are worth it when someone pays you a compliment. It is marvelously well-mannered to learn how to graciously accept a compliment instead of swatting it away like a pesky fly. When someone says something nice to you, like, "that was an excellent presentation", do not wave the compliment away by noting that you missed a slide, stumbled on the introduction, messed up your close or the like. Doing so gives the impression that you are insecure and don't think you deserve a compliment. You do deserve a compliment! Life can be pretty tough from time to time. Don't make it more difficult by rejecting the kindnesses that are given to you. Whenever someone gives you a heartfelt compliment, you should smile and simply say, "Thank you."

The same advice applies to situations when someone thanks you. Don't dismiss their gratitude with "it was nothing". Instead, smile and say, "you're welcome."

Applying this in the real world

Q. My colleague always tells me how pretty I look. It makes me uncomfortable and I don't want to say, "Thank you." I just want them to stop.

A. Being well-mannered does not mean being a doormat and being made to feel uncomfortable at work. The next time your colleague offers up a compliment (and you think your colleague is friendly and otherwise appropriate), calmly explain that you know they intend to be nice with the compliment, but you would prefer they not talk about your looks. You are at work and want to be known for your skills and intellect and not distract others with your appearance. If, on the other hand, you think your colleague is more on the creepy side, look them in the eye and clearly say, "Please don't comment on my looks anymore. It makes me uncomfortable." They may try to put all the blame on you and act like you are over-reacting. Don't fall for it. Stay calm and say, "I asked you to stop. I expect you to do so. Now let's get back to work." If they don't stop, your next stop is HR. No one should be made to feel uncomfortable at work.

Q. Whenever someone compliments me on something, should I return one in the same conversation?

A. Compliments should be genuine. Compliments are not ping pong balls intended to be batted back and forth. We all know an insincere compliment when we hear one so don't peddle those. Never return a compliment just for the sake of doing so. Instead, respect the other person enough to graciously accept their compliment with a "thank you" and a smile. Making others feel good is such a treat. Don't deny them that feeling when they said something nice about you.

6

Polite Self-Control is Marvelous and Freeing

"If you can be patient in one moment of anger, you will escape 100 days of sorrow."—CHINESE PROVERB

Never was there a truer statement. When you lose your temper or patience and lash out at someone, you disrespect yourself and those you encounter–you are rude and not marvelously well-mannered. Angry outbursts will adversely impact your career, particularly if your boss, colleague, or client sees them. They will lose trust in you and your ability to control your temper and well-represent your organization. No one wants a hothead around.

When you lose control, you act in a way that might make you feel good for that fleeting moment ("Boy, I showed them!"), but upon reflection, makes you feel awfully bad about yourself and embarrassed about your dreadful behavior. You think, "That wasn't really me, that isn't how I want to act, that is not how I want the world to view me." Boom, in an instant, you are mad at yourself.

Was it worth it? We think not. Polite self-control makes you marvelously well-mannered and happy. How marvelous, but sometimes how difficult.

Acting politely won't constrain your ability to self-express–"I need to be me". Being polite and purposeful in your actions actually places you in absolute control of your behavior, your personal brand, and, ultimately, your well-being. You feel good about yourself when you are at your best and showcasing the "self" that you want to others to see. On the converse, reacting without any regard for others is to be out of control, self-centered, and self-indulgent, and, dare we say, spoiled. That certainly is not the personal best you want to parade around for others to see, is it?

It takes adult self-restraint to affirmatively choose to be civil and polite, even when faced with situations that make our blood boil. Rude sales clerk? Check. Crazy driver who cuts in front of us? Check. Squabbling children? Check. Sneaky work colleague taking credit for your work? Check. There is an endless supply of people or situations that can bring out the worst in you–if you let them.

By being polite and in control, and by exercising some self-restraint and self-editing, we are making the affirmative choice to act in a way that leads us to happiness and self-respect[23]. It means choosing to act so that we will feel better fifteen minutes from now. You want to feel good after the storm passes. Our manners and self-control calm us in any situation, which really is freeing ourselves from feeling bad!

So, stop being a five-minute anger adrenaline junkie!

Applying this in the real world

Q. How can I control my anger so that I don't have outbursts?

A. It takes practice. Some people count to ten. Some people walk away. Some people take three deep breaths before responding. Some people pinch their own fingers or clench their palms. We like to imagine that someone is literally handing us an invitation to lose our cool, get angry, and be rude. That is certainly not the type of "invitation" we feel like accepting, so we flick our wrist and wave off the invitation. We politely decline the invitation to lose control and be rude.

Q. How do I express my anger is a mature way?

A. Anger is a normal emotion. Everyone gets angry. When you are angry, it is important to deliberately control your reaction by speaking only after you have taken a moment or two to calm down. Try not to raise your voice or use harsh words when communicating your displeasure.

How to Reject Invitations to Rudeness Without Being a Doormat at Work

"Treat everyone with politeness, even those who are rude to you—not because they are nice, but because you are."
– UNKNOWN

It is easy to be polite when everyone is nice, isn't it? Sure it is, because kindness generally begets kindness. But not everyone is polite. Sooner or later, you will encounter a dud. We define a dud as someone who is rude and offensive. For example, what do you do when you are in a meeting and a colleague is needlessly rude, disparages your work, or otherwise tries to take you down a peg or two in the eyes of your other co-workers and your boss? Your first impulse may be to respond with your own rudeness, but don't.

When work colleagues—or anyone else you encounter - act rudely, don't engage in retaliatory rudeness. That is what they want. They want to get you to engage, so purposefully disengage. **Reject their invitation to be angry.** Say, "No thank you."

So, if you're rejecting the invitation to be angry, what do you actually do?

You don't want to just *take it*. Don't worry, we aren't going to tell you to do that. Being polite doesn't mean being a doormat. When politeness is part of your brand, you don't sink to the level of rude people. You respect yourself and your environment enough to act appropriately and with proper adult self-restraint. In times like this, remember to **SMOVE**–smile and move on.

So, what does SMOVING look like? Well, let's say you are at a work cocktail reception and you realize you are talking to a dud who just offended you with an inappropriate joke or comment. You first offer a tight-lipped smile to subtly indicate your displeasure. Next, you speak a simple phrase in a calm voice that indicates you are leaving such as, "I see my colleague and I need to go talk to her before she leaves. Please excuse me." Then turn and walk away. Proximity breeds trouble, so physically put some distance between you and the offending party. If you think this person is a dud, your whole body will be sending messages that you don't like this cat, so get away from them. Don't let them control you or the situation you are in. You must maintain and exercise control and you do that by walking away.

Here's another example. Let's go back to that meeting where your colleague is passively aggressive, trying to bring you down a peg or two in the eyes of the others at the meeting. SMOVE here too but note it does not entail leaving the meeting. Sometimes the best SMOVE response is a deliberate, pregnant pause and a long glance at them before promptly turning your attention to the others in the meeting with a smile and deliberately engaging in the agenda at hand. Or you may calmly state, "do not (state the offending conduct) toward me" and tie the impact of their rude behavior back to work. Then direct your smile and engagement to the others at the table. You will look professional, calm, cool, and collected–and unruffled. The dud, on the other hand, will just look unprofessional.

Applying this in the real world

Q. When someone is rude to me, why can't I call them out on the carpet and give them a snide response to put them in their place?

A. Don't fall into the trap of feeling that the dud's rudeness justifies yours. Sorry, there is no free pass on bad manners. Don't be part of the cycle. Be marvelously well-mannered and remember to "be nice to everyone, even rude people, not because they are nice but because you are." The only thing you can control in a sticky situation is your own reaction. You can stand your ground and politely move on.

Q. Isn't ignoring someone at a meeting letting them walk all over you?

A. SMOVE does not mean ignore. It means that you respect yourself and your environment enough to act appropriately. If you can calmly articulate the conduct you object to, then do so, even in the presence of others.

The Art of the Apology

People are human. People make mistakes. And when they do, they usually give an apology.

How often have we seen a celebrity apologizing for cheating on a spouse, or a public figure apologizing for inappropriate or unethical behavior, and the like? Many of these public apologies have not been all that stellar. Thankfully–to date–when we have had to make an apology, it has always been in private, without the world watching. And instead of critiquing us, the people we have apologized to have usually been top-drawer and extremely gracious in accepting our heartfelt apologies. We have been very lucky. Sooner or later, everyone needs to apologize. So, what constitutes a good apology?

As the title of this chapter notes, an apology is an art, not a science. There is no strict formula that automatically grants you dispensation for your mistake. Knowing how to give a good apology is an essential skill, both in our personal and our professional lives. We are all human and, therefore, imperfect. We all make mistakes for which we should apologize. When someone can't or won't apologize, it says something about their character–or lack thereof. And others take note.

People don't want your apology if you aren't sorry. But if you are truly sorry, there is a way to convey it in a heartfelt apology. It is important to be specific in what you are apologizing for. You need to mention what you did–the actual act or deed. **Do not say, "I**

am sorry if you feel that…". That is *not* an apology. That sort of "apology" implies that you think they are over-sensitive and you're sorry only that their feelings got hurt. It implies that the blame is on them–not you. You need to say that you regret what you did and then you need to ask for forgiveness and ask what, if anything, there is that you can do to make the situation better.

While no apology is the same as the next–the cast of characters and situations change–the previously mentioned elements, coupled with doing an apology *without delay*, certainly help. However, a late apology (sometimes when cooler heads prevail) is certainly better than an apology never made.

While it's important to offer the apology, it is also important to remember that you cannot control if your apology will be accepted. You can only control whether you give a sincere apology with grace. If done well, you will improve your relationships and reputation, as well as mend fences[24]. Please keep in mind, if your apology is not immediately accepted, you must not get angry. That will not help the situation. Just because you are ready to give an apology does not mean someone is ready to accept it. You don't get to dictate the timetable. If this happens to you, we recommend trying again at another time. Then you will have done all you can and are able to proceed with a clean conscious.

A sincere apology is evidence of strength of character, not of weakness. Giving a good apology makes you marvelously well-mannered and makes you feel good. Pure and simple.

Applying this in the real world

Q. I would like to apologize when I know I am wrong, but I tend to avoid it out of pride.

A. Apologizing is hard because we have to admit we did something wrong and acknowledge we caused offense and pain. It isn't easy to admit such weakness. But in cases like this, it is easier on you if you just do it. As soon as you know you did something wrong, speak up with sincerity. The person you hurt will feel better sooner, as will you.

Q. A colleague always says to me, "I am sorry you feel that…". It makes me feel like I am in the wrong. What can I do?

A. No one likes to be blamed for feeling offended. If you are not always looking to be offended by this person, but they seem to repeatedly do things that bother you, speak up. You can choose not to accept their apology by saying, "I really don't feel as though my feelings are the problem here but rather it is (insert their transgression)." Then, if you want to move past it, you can follow up with, "what can we do about that so we can prevent this from happening again?" Then listen to what they are willing to try. Ideally, they will come up with a plan that works for you and the relationship can mend. Or you can end the conversation with your first comment, which lets them know the apology has not been accepted. Just keep in mind, they may not try to apologize again, and if you want to repair the relationship, the next step may very well have to be yours.

Self-Respect Leads to Respect of Others

It is important to respect yourself. You can't be anyone else, so it's best to learn to embrace and cherish yourself. All you can do is work on becoming the best version of yourself, so focus on becoming a person you like and can be proud of. It is important for you to start treating yourself with the kindness and consideration you more freely show others.

When you behave with dignity and grace, you know you are acting appropriately. Take pride in the moments you behave well because it's hard to always be proud of your words and deeds.

In order to truly respect yourself, you must approve of the life you're living. You need to make good choices. Do the right thing even when it's hard. You need to be comfortable being uncomfortable for the few minutes it takes to make a difficult but good choice so that you can feel proud of your actions after the fact. There will be many moments in life when you need to make the right—and difficult—choice. When you fail to do so, you will remember those moments with regret.

Act to avoid regret.

It feels good to be proud of your actions. The more you feel this way, the easier it is to continue to make good choices.

Part of making good choices is surrounding yourself with good people. Cut the fat—those who aren't making good choices. You deserve to be treated well by others—and by yourself.

Treating yourself well is not about ego or self-esteem. Feeling better about yourself (so you can treat yourself well) requires being proud of your character and respecting yourself means treating yourself with dignity and grace. You do this by bestowing on yourself the kindness, patience, and understanding you so easily give to others. Give yourself a break. When you treat yourself well, it shows. People take note and will treat you better in return. Because you are indeed worth it. When you don't like yourself, that also shows, and people take note of that fact too—and act accordingly.

Once you respect yourself, you can truly respect other people as well. When you respect other people, you don't act entitled. You are grateful for all your blessings, including your relationships with other people. When you are grateful, the little things roll off your back, making you more likeable and enjoyable to be around. Consciously try to develop a grateful outlook. You will enjoy a better well-being as a result.

Let's face it, no one likes to be around a Debbi-Downer or Negative-Nelly or Snobby-Sam. A great place to start is to say, "Thank you," more often, and really mean it. No act of kindness is too small to show gratitude toward. Indeed, those small moments have a big impact.

"The best portion of a good man's life: his little, nameless unremembered acts of kindness and love."
— WILLIAM WORDSWORTH

It is also important for your brand to always treat others well, even when you know it might not be reciprocated. You must respect yourself enough not to sink to their level. You are better than that. You control your own behavior and ***never*** cede that control to someone else.

Applying this in the real world

Q. How do I understand who my "self" is so that I can focus on creating an accurate, sustainable brand? It's hard to be someone I'm not.

A. It is important to truly understand who you are–and the goal is to be the best version of yourself. That is our goal in crafting an intentional brand. It is not to be someone completely different. That would be exhausting. To help create your brand, look at the personality traits you possess (ex. Are you an Introvert/ Extrovert? Serious/Jokester? Positive/Negative?). These are typically engrained in you, so find ways to make them work for you–not against you. Then review your character traits (ex. Kind? Honest? Helpful? Moral?). With hard work, all of us can improve our character. Taken together, these steps will help you understand who you are and what you are capable of becoming.

Q. How can I "trim the fat", so to speak, at work and only associate with other people of character?

A. It is rare for us to be able to choose the people we get to work with. You can, however, limit their ability to adversely impact you. Don't engage with gossipers. Document your communications and interactions with people who you view as untrustworthy. Try to only interact with those people in the presence of a third person. Be polite, professional, and keep your distance when you can.

Have Good Character and Keep Your Word

"You're only as good as your word and your word is only as good as your action." - UNKNOWN

You need to follow through if you want to have a solid personal brand. That means your actions need to match your words, no two ways about it. All of the following represent a lack of follow-through:

- "I'll get back to you on that"–then you let the email chain die.
- "Let's do lunch"–then you don't follow up to make actual plans.
- "I can get that done by morning"–then you blow through the deadline.
- RSVP to an event–then are a no show.

In practice, follow-through means answering emails, following up on requests, returning calls and texts, and the like. If you make a commitment, you need to keep it so that your words have value. A promise is a commitment to yourself as well as to others. When you don't keep your word, you are letting the other person know that you don't value them and you don't value your *own* word. They learn not to count on you. You learn not to count on you. Both relationships suffer, and so does your overall personal brand.

Under-promise and over-deliver. Only commit to what you know you can fulfill. Then work hard to fulfill it. Just do it. Put effort in everything you do, no matter how small the task. When you practice that daily effort, your personal brand starts to include the important ingredient of good character.

> *"People with good intentions make promises.*
> *People with good character keep them."* – UNKNOWN

Consistency and authenticity are important in developing a personal brand. You can't try to be someone you are not. You can only try to become the very best version of the person you *are meant to be.*

One thing that is important for your brand is that you not be a gossip. **Do not speak ill of others**. When you do, others wonder what you say about *them* when they are not around. Be kind in your words. Use the magic words often: "please", "thank you", "you're welcome" and, "I'm sorry".

It is important not to play with your **integrity**–knowing right from wrong and acting accordingly. You need to protect it. Be honest. Do not cheat, lie, or steal. These faults will only disappoint you and inhibit your ability to like yourself and treat yourself well.

You should consistently reinforce your personal brand in all your activities–face-to-face meetings, networking events, business lunches and dinners, and receptions–along with everyone you encounter, such as colleagues, clients, subordinates, and bosses. You should consistently reinforce your personal brand across all your digital platforms when you choose to be active with those platforms.

With so many digital platforms and other technology, worlds are colliding. The professional and personal lines are blurring. Those blurring lines mean you should display the same characteristics in both worlds. Although it might sound exhausting trying to "always be on", we aren't telling you to "always be on". What we are telling you is to **be consistent and true to yourself** at all times, across your personal and professional lives. When you do that, you aren't really ever "on". You are just you. And then, it is quite easy. You are simply working to consistently and truly be the kindest and best version of yourself.

When you follow the rules of etiquette and act well-mannered as part of your brand, you will have a quiet confidence that comes with knowing what to do, when to do it, and how to do it well. You will be more relaxed and start enjoying yourself. Then you can focus on other people because you aren't worrying about yourself. When you focus on others, you end up being more engaging and enjoyable to be around. You make others feel included and welcomed in your presence. And when you do that, people will start seeking you out. Having consistently good character is truly a win-win situation.

Applying this in the real world

Q. My boss always wants me to fudge numbers in a regular report to clients. I am uncomfortable. What should I do?

A. This is a difficult situation. You should re-evaluate if that is the type of person you want to work for. In the meantime, clearly and firmly state your objection, document your work meticulously, and speak to someone in higher management or HR.

Q. I am the "queen of good intentions". I mean to follow through, but I have trouble. What can I do?

A. You need to joyfully just do it. Keep track of your obligations and commitments and fulfill them if you want your word to have meaning. This may mean that you need to learn to politely say "no" more often. While you want to help, if you don't have the bandwidth at the time, simply say no. This helps you to avoid disappointing someone to whom you have already made a commitment. Writing down your obligations in a to-do list or setting digital reminders for yourself is a great way to make sure you follow through.

PART II

BUSINESS ETIQUETTE.

Good for <u>Your</u> Business

One rarely succeeds in business alone. You need other people. Not only that, but you also need to work well with other people–support staff, subordinates, colleagues, bosses, customers, and clients. You need their support if you are going to contribute and do your job well.

When you learn the rules of business etiquette, they become part of you. You gain a quiet confidence when you know what to do, how to do it, and when to do it. You don't have to second guess yourself and be paralyzed by insecurity. With this confidence comes the freedom to focus on both making others feel welcome in your presence and on the work agenda at hand. Business etiquette is paramount to your professional success.

What Does Sex
Have to Do With it?

Many gentlemen were taught to be deferential to ladies by holding doors, pulling out chairs, and waiting for ladies to extend a hand before extending theirs. The foundational rule of "ladies first" is found in traditional social etiquette. However, things are different in the business world.

Gender does not matter in business. When you work with women, they are your colleagues. When you work for a woman, she is your boss or client. When you manage a woman, she is part of your staff. Nothing more and nothing less.

The business etiquette rule for handshakes is that you **extend your hand first**. Do not wait for a lady or someone more senior to do it. When you extend your hand first, it signals that you are confident. It benefits your personal brand. Do it even if you are extending your hand first to a lady. Please see Chapter 14 for a complete discussion of handshakes.

The business etiquette rule for introductions is that you say the "more important person's" name first and say you would like to introduce "to you" the name of the other person. Ladies can be introduced to men. Power and precedence determine whose name is said first, not gender. Please see Chapter 15 for a complete discussion of business introductions.

The business etiquette rule for holding doors is that you **hold the door for whomever comes after you**–lady or gentleman. Regardless of whether they have their hands full. When you are going through a revolving door, you should go ahead of your client, the more senior person (based on power and precedence), or someone who may need an extra hand, so that you may start pushing the door for them. As you approach the revolving door say, "Please let me go in first so that I can push the door." Then proceed into the revolving door and greet them on the other side after they make their way through.

The business etiquette rule for utilizing real estate in business meetings is that everyone is entitled to the same amount of space around the conference table. Sit up straight, take a seat, and place your materials on the table space that goes with your seat. Use your body to exude confidence with good posture, a smile, and looking prepared to participate. You belong in the meeting–you were invited, right? Of course! **Do not try to fold yourself up and take up less space**. That signals insecurity. Likewise, do not over-spread trying to look confident and important. You only look insecure and arrogant.

The business etiquette rule for dining is that a gentleman need not help a lady with her chair. If he does, the lady should simply smile and say, "Thank you," for the kindness, as opposed to acting offended at the help.

Applying this in the real world

Q. I want to take up my real estate at meetings, but the guys always take up all the room at the table.

A. Get to the meeting earlier than at least one of them and place your materials on the table. This is a great time to connect with the other attendees before the meeting. If someone tries to encroach on your table space, politely say, "Excuse me. My things are there. Please do not touch them. I need them for the meeting." Smile and hold your ground.

Q. I was raised to always be deferential to the lady. I find it difficult and uncomfortable to not do so, even in business.

A. You sound very polite and well-mannered. But remember that being well-mannered means making others feel comfortable and welcome. By doing this in the workplace, you may be making *them* uncomfortable. If there is a lady with whom you work who you know appreciates these niceties, feel free to continue to do it, but in general treat your colleagues the same, regardless of gender.

12

Be a Connecting Navigator

The goal here is to intentionally create a group of acquaintances and associates that you keep active through regular and meaningful communication for mutual benefit. Given that no one succeeds alone in business–or very few people do–you should learn to connect with other people so you can create your own professional cheering squad. To be successful, approach "connecting" by thinking, "How can I help, what can I offer" not "what can I get from them". It makes it easier for you if you think about the other person. You feel less slick or like you are using people.

To connect well, you need to do your job well so that you have something to offer the other person in terms of your experience, your advice, your knowledge, and your willingness to share your professional connections. Connecting people and information-sharing is not code for a gossiping coffee-klatch. You want to share thoughtful information and help make a difference in someone else's career. When you peddle in gossip, you may think you look "in the know" but you are just letting others know that you are indiscrete and have bad judgment–characteristics that will not aid your professional advancement.

Everyone can spot "an operator", so don't act like one. Instead, you want to be genuine in your interactions with others. Realize relationship-building takes time. You want to foster relationships, not force them. Forcing relationships just makes others uncomfortable.

Instead, look for opportunities to touch base with those in your networking orbit by sharing useful information, making yourself available for advice and counsel, or helping them connect with people you know.

Once you connect with someone, it is important to make sure you don't let the relationship go cold or stale from neglect. To avoid this, get organized and develop a system that works for your schedule and your workload. The key is to make sure you regularly touch base with people in your circle of support. For example, if you catch up on reading every weekend, on Monday mornings you may find it easy to forward relevant articles to a handful of people to let them know you are thinking of them and thought they would find the information helpful. Or you may be someone who has the flexibility to take a long coffee break every Thursday afternoon. Consider scheduling to meet someone on those coffee breaks. Or you may be someone who regularly attends industry luncheons and you are able to invite a guest. If that is the case, give thought to inviting someone from your networking circle. Spending quality face-to-face time with your cheering squad is important.

Of course, knowing what to do once you've met someone is great, but how do you meet them in the first place?

Well, one of the easiest places to begin creating a connecting orbit is at a work event. You already have work in common and that's a start. Conversely, those events can also be the hardest because most of us don't mingle with ease. It is said that upwards of 75 percent of adults experience anxiety attending events with strangers. If that describes you, you're not alone! Don't worry, we are going to share with you what you need to know to survive and thrive at these events by properly navigating the room.

First things first, wear a name badge if it is provided. It helps others identify you and helps you identify others. It is properly placed on your upper right shoulder. Ladies, you may want to invest in your own magnetic nametag that you can take from event to event. It protects your clothes from pin holes and allows you to wear clothes (typically dresses) that are difficult to clip on a name badge too. Avoid long lanyards at all costs–otherwise people will be gazing at your navel area!

The key is to view these work events–like an industry conference, or luncheon or reception–like any other work meeting you attend during the day. When you go to a meeting, you prepare (or you should). The same applies here. Prepare, prepare, prepare. Spend some time doing advance work before the event. Brief yourself. If, for example, you are attending an industry cocktail reception, ask yourself, who is going to be there? What is the agenda? Who do you want to see? What do you want to say to them? When you do your "homework" before the event, you will be more confident at the event. And that confidence will show.

Start making yourself stand out in a good way when you first enter the reception room. Don't scurry in and immediately head towards the canapés, crudité, and cocktails. You can eat and drink at these events, but you don't want that to be your main mission. In fact, you should have a bite to eat before you get there! A hungry or tipsy connecting navigator is not the best. Avoid messy foods and opt for one-bite appetizers on toothpicks to keep your fingers clean. Always take the cocktail napkin when you take the food. Also, be mindful of the "never-ending" wine glass if wait-staff is automatically refilling glasses. You may think you only went up to the bar once when you really had four glasses of wine. You never want to be an embarrassment to yourself, your organization, or the host. That is bad for your personal brand. When you are having a drink, hold the glass in your left hand to keep your right one free and dry for handshakes.

Always be gracious. Walk in with good posture and a smile, and once you enter the room, step aside and pause. This lets all the people watching the door to spot you looking confident and in control as you get your bearings. Take a breath, pause, and survey the room with a smile. People are drawn to confident and friendly people, so act that way. You were invited. You belong. Act like it.

Next you need to read the room and the people in it[25]. When you read the room, you are looking to determine the energy of the room. You want to conform your own energy to it. If the event is lively and full of energy, you want to ramp your own energy up as well. Likewise, if it is a more quiet and subdued affair, you want to adjust your demeanor accordingly. The goal is to have your energy and demeanor match the room so that you look like you belong.

After reading the room, you need to figure out who to talk too. You can always look for individuals standing by themselves. They would love it if you would go up and introduce yourself and start a conversation. Show some kindness and save them from solitude. You can also look for groups of three or more who look friendly–ones that are smiling, have open stances, and occasionally look around the room and make eye-contact with folks passing by. If they are doing those things, they are signaling that they are nice and approachable.

You should avoid going up to two people talking (unless you know them). They are likely facing each other and not making eye contact with those passing by. They are concentrating on each other, so don't invade their conversation. Likewise, you should not approach groups that look like the life of the party. If you see a group that is high-fiving, laughing loudly at jokes, etc., proceed with extreme caution. While they may look like a ton of fun, they aren't likely to welcome a stranger because you are going to change the group's dynamic and rhythm. They are already a cohesive group.

Applying this in the real world

Q. I recently was at an event where everyone was paired up talking except for one group of 3-4 people but they weren't sending signals of inclusion. They didn't look like a group that was even marginally enjoying themselves. What should I have done?

A. The group would have been the only viable option. You can approach groups that don't look like they are clicking. But when you do, you need to put effort into enlivening the group. That group would have likely benefited from some additional, new energy. Act confident by putting on a smile, standing tall, and extending your hand and introducing yourself.

Q. You said not to immediately head to the food or drink. When can I?

A. Food and drink are served at these events. Your host wants you to partake. Most people immediately head to the bar or buffet because they don't know what else to do. Before you do that, survey the room, see who is there that you know, and see if you can locate those you have targeted to meet. Make one of those connections first, then you can end the conversation and head to the bar. Cheers, a new connection has been made! Now make sure to follow up.

13

Be Quiet and Learn How to be a Great Conversationalist

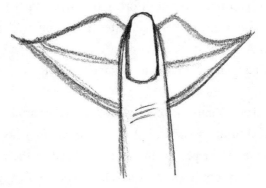

Once you have found someone to talk with, you need to talk. In your conversation, you want to signal that you are non-threatening, approachable, and kind. Small talk is your goal. Small talk is conversation about non-sensitive topics and is a conversation starter–not stopper. It allows relationships to take root and blossom in a non-threatening way.

Before a word comes out of your mouth, let's review your deportment. As you may recall, your body is constantly talking to the world.

What is it saying?

When you meet someone new, you want to have a welcoming stance. No crossed arms, no slouching. You should smile, nod when you are listening to others, and maintain eye contact. You want your body to communicate positively with others.

Now for what to actually say. Small talk becomes easier when you are up on current events. Read your industry trades, national newspaper, magazines, or your local paper before an event. Another great option is to subscribe to a news source so that you can skim the news first thing in the morning. Your opinions of some celebrities and reality stars aside, pop culture is fine to talk about. You want the conversation to be easy. So, in addition to talking about the event—"what did you think of the keynote speech?" "how do you know the host", "what panel are you most looking forward to"—you want the conversation to **FLOW** as much as possible[26]. Here are some topic ideas to get the other person engaged in a conversation.

F–family, friends and Fido (pets). "Do you have plans with friends and family over the upcoming holiday break?" "I saw the cutest dog at the airport on my way to the conference, do you have any pets?"

L–leisure activities like hobbies and sports. "Are you following the US Open (or insert seasonal sporting event or team here)?", "Do you do any winter sports?"

O–occupation or what else occupies your time. "What's your biggest challenge at work now?" "How does Y announcement impact your company's plans?" "Wow your passion for X is amazing. Do you have a side gig or do any philanthropic work that involves X."

W–who, what, where, when and why. "What do you think companies can do to improve their cyber-security?" "What are you presenting at the conference tomorrow?" The beauty of asking W questions is that they get the other person talking and prevent (in most cases) someone being able to respond with a simple "yes" or "no".

When you are talking with someone, the goal is to focus on them and make them feel important so look them in the eye. Do not look over their shoulder to find someone more important. Do not check your texts. Focus on the person in front of you. You want to be an active listener: restate what you hear (instead of thinking of what you can say next), nod to show you are listening, and ask follow-up questions. Don't interrupt or complete others' thoughts for them. Let them finish what they want to say. Be patient and interested. We know this can be hard when you are enthused to be engaged in a great conversation, but patience pays off.

When engaged in small talk, remember that people love to talk about themselves so work hard not to monopolize the conversation, start every sentence with "I" (so boring!), or try to top their story with your own (so boorish!). "You just went to Italy? So did we ..." then you proceed to go on a seven-minute monologue on your *fabulous* vacation. Instead, you should have said, "You went to Italy? I love Italy. What was your favorite site?" See what we did here? We let them know we were listening by restating what they just said ("went to Italy") and then we asked *them* a follow-up question ("What was your favorite site?"). By signaling that we know a thing or two about Italy ("I love Italy"), we have given them a hook on what to ask us next to keep the conversation going in dialogue form rather than monologue. How marvelous!

Some things not to talk about include health issues, religion, and gossip. Small talk is to signal you are friend not foe, kind not cruel, respectable not rude, tasteful not tasteless. Talking about serious health issues, religion or gossiping with anyone (let alone someone you just met) sends the message that you are either choosing not to be appropriate or don't know how to act appropriately in a business setting.

When you want to end the conversation, don't feel bad. The key is to be confident and kind. Remember small talk is just that–small. It is supposed to only be 10-15 minutes–just long enough to establish you are good people and start to build a relationship. You are supposed to mingle with others so don't feel bad, just wind down the conversation. Smile, have a phrase ready to end the conversation, offer to exchange business cards, and shake hands and walk away. Easy, breezy.

Applying this in the real world

Q. Ending a conversation is always so awkward for me. Help!

A. Small talk is not supposed to be long. You and everyone else at these types of work events are looking to network and meet new people. To help you politely close down a conversation, practice a few closing phrases and have them ready. "It was so nice meeting you, but I need to re-connect with my colleague. I hope to see you soon, may I give you my card?" or "It was a delight talking with you, but I need to say my thanks to the host before I leave, may I give you my card?" or "I really enjoyed talking with you. I would love to continue but I need to get back to my client/boss/ etc. May I give you my card?". Said confidently and with a smile, these conversation closers are relationship starters. If they give you their card, follow up and you are off to the races!

Q. I can never think of anything to say after I introduce myself. What should I do?

A. Read trade magazines or an article or two in the newspaper. Think of a book you just read, museum exhibit-opening you just attended, movie you just saw, or a sporting event you just watched. Remember, asking a W question should get the other person talking.

14

Please Take My Hand

Shaking hands is important in business. Back in the day one would extend their hand to show a new person that they were friendly and didn't bear arms. Today you shake hands to show that you are friendly and approachable. You shake hands when you meet someone for the first time, when you enter a room and approach people you know, or they approach you, and when you exit a conversation. In business, you extend your hand first because it signals confidence, remember? The goal is to look gracious when you shake hands.

Handshakes are the physical greeting that accompany your words and, as we discussed in the Deportment chapter, your body sends messages. Likewise, your handshakes do too.

Bad handshakes send bad messages. We all have experienced a bad handshake:

- The hand hug–where someone clasps your hand in both of theirs–sends the signal that someone is insincere and trying to force intimacy.
- The princess or limp fish handshake–where someone doesn't give a whole, firm hand for you to shake–sends the signal that someone doesn't care to meet you and is not engaged.
- The bone-crusher handshake–where someone tries to squeeze your knuckles together–sends the signal that someone is aggressive and insecure.

No one likes to be on the receiving end of those handshakes so let's make sure you don't give one. A proper handshake is given while standing and is comprised of five easy steps:

1. Mirror the other person by facing them and squaring your shoulders with theirs, lining up your hips with theirs, and pointing your toes towards theirs.
2. Smile as you extend your hand with your thumb up and fingers straight and out. Let the other person grip your hand and connect (palm to palm) for a complete handshake.
3. Grip their hand so that you achieve web to web contact. The areas between the thumb and index finger of both hands should connect.
4. Shake from the elbow. Do not wriggle your wrist or awkwardly move your shoulder.
5. Do two to three graceful pumps with your hands clasped together and then release. Gently drop your arm down to your side while maintaining a smile.

If someone does not extend their hand when you extend yours, don't fret. It is about them, not you. They could have arthritis, they could have a cold (thank you for not spreading germs), they could be a germaphobe, or they could have some other religious or cultural reason. You don't know, and you don't control that. What you *can* control is your reaction. Maintain your composure and pull your arm and hand back to your side as you maintain your smile and continue talking.

Sometimes a person might respond to your extended hand not with theirs, but by folding their arm up and holding their fist over their heart with a slight bow toward you. That is their "handshake" and it is appropriate for you to mirror it.

Applying this in the real world

Q. What do I do when I want to shake hands, but someone goes in for a hug–someone I don't want to hug?

A. If you know someone is a serial hugger, you need to beat them to the punch by extending your hand quickly while keeping your distance so that you don't get in range of a hug. This takes finesse. Keep smiling (you want to look friendly) and keep your hand firmly out to serve as a bit of a body block. Take a slight step back or lean back so you are out of their "hug" reach. Keep in mind that if you are doing business in another country, it may be a part of their business culture to hug. You should do what is appropriate in the country you are working in. In the US, handshakes are the norm, not hugs and kisses.

Q. I have tendinitis and find it difficult to shake hands when it flairs up. What should I do?

A. Health and safety first. If your hand hurts, you should not shake hands but rather politely smile and do one of the following alternatives: wear a hand brace and say, "It's so nice to meet you, please excuse me but I cannot shake hands at the moment"; hold something else like a pen in your hand and extend your left hand instead as you say your verbal greeting; or place your closed fist over your heart and offer a slight bow as you provide your verbal greeting. It is entirely up to you whether or not you explain that you aren't shaking hands because of your health obstacle.

May I Please Introduce to You...

It is your job to represent yourself well in business. Part of that means being able to introduce yourself. Despite knowing their name and where they work, many people have a difficult time introducing themselves. Just think back to the last gathering you were at where everyone went around introducing themselves. We guarantee that many said their names so quickly and quietly that you had to strain to catch what they were saying.

If you have a long name, a multi-syllable name, or a name that is difficult to pronounce, don't make it harder on the person you are speaking to by rushing through your name. Say your name slowly enough, clearly enough, and loudly enough so that the other person can hear your name and record it in their mind. They want to know your name so they can use it in the future. The last thing they want to do is ask you to repeat your name. Help them out. Help yourself out. Savor every syllable of your name and watch your pace, tone, and clarity. Love your name.

Well-done.

Introducing other people is a bit trickier, but if you master this skill it conveys a great deal of confidence. It is a skill that you simply must learn as you will most likely have to introduce someone else at least once in your career. Once you learn to do it–only by practicing–you will get better at it. The better you are at it, the more you will enjoy doing it and the more you will do it. Soon you will get a reputation for being generous with your contacts. You will be known for bringing people together and making them feel welcome. Developing this skill will help you become a "connector" (discussed in Chapter 12). People will soon be seeking you out at events for introductions. We promise.

Here is the formula for introducing others:

MIP's Name + "To You" + Junior Person's Name

Hence, a proper business introduction would sound like this:

"Larry, I would like to introduce <u>to you</u> Sara Morris, our new summer associate. Sara, please meet Larry Sidman, a partner at our firm."

You should notice a few things with this introduction. **The MIP– the More Important Person's–name is said first.** By the time the introduction is complete, both individuals' **first and last names have been said**. This is a balanced introduction.

Adding a bit of information about each person gives them the context of why they are being introduced. You want to avoid "introduction ping pong" by only saying their names. Had you said, "Larry meet Sara, Sara meet Larry," they would have looked at you as if you had three heads. They would have no idea why you were introducing them or how to start small talk without relying on you. That is an introduction fail. Instead, you told them what each other's roles were at the firm. If you had to then excuse yourself, those two could have easily engaged in some small talk. Larry could ask Sara what projects she was working on or where she goes to law school, while Sara could ask Larry what practice group he was in and how long he had been at the firm. You would look like a rock star and those two would have started a pleasant conversation. That is an introduction win.

Again, always say the more important person's name first and make sure to follow it with the phrase, "I would like to introduce *to you*". "To you" is key. You are giving the MIP the gift of an introduction. So just like you sing "happy birthday TO YOU" you introduce "TO YOU". If you switch it around to "you to" you end up changing who you are introducing to whom and that is incorrect. When following up with the second part of the introduction, say the Junior Person's name followed by "please meet".

You need to quickly decide which person is the MIP so you don't miss the opportunity to do the introduction in the first place. Some rules of thumb for business introductions are:

- Gender doesn't matter in business–the one with the power is the MIP
- Public Officials are the MIP
- When introducing two individuals in the private sector, follow the normal pecking order of a business–C-suite over middle management over entry level employees
- Your customer or client is always the MIP even when the other person is your CEO

And when in doubt, simply quickly decide who the MIP is and do the introduction with a smile and confident tone.

Applying this in the real world

Q. People often mispronounce my name. I feel badly correcting them.

A. No, don't feel badly! They want to know the proper way to say your name. Correct them. Simply smile and say, "Actually my name is..." And if this happens often, it is a sign that you are probably not saying your name slowly, clearly, or loudly enough for them to catch it. Also, if people shorten your name—say from Jennifer to Jen or Christopher to Chris and you don't like that, smile and say, "Actually, I go by (insert full name)." Correct them every time until they get it right. But do so kindly—not with irritation.

Q. I stumble every time I try to introduce someone.

A. You just have to practice. Pure and simple. This is a skill that must be learned. And practice makes perfect. Practice introducing people (following the business rules above) in social settings where you feel more confident. The more you do it, the better you will be at it.

Hey You!

THE ART OF REMEMBERING NEW NAMES

Many people have difficulty remembering names when meeting a lot of new people at the same time. The best thing to do is slow down and focus. By this, we mean listen to the other person. Oftentimes, in trying to make a good first impression, we are so busy thinking of what we want to say next that we neglect to listen to the other person and miss the moment when they introduce themselves to us. You will make a better impression by being present in the conversation, and you are present when you listen.

Once someone introduces themselves, immediately repeat back their name, "It's nice to meet you, Jennifer." Then try to say the person's name an additional time or two during the conversation so that you reinforce it in your mind. However, be careful not to overdo it. If you pepper the conversation with the continuous mention of their name, they will think you are a bit off, so it's best to limit it to one or two times.

As you mentally file away their name, try to associate their name with an adjective that suits your first impression of that person–Funny Frank, Cool Claire, etc. Engaging in lively small talk will help you figure out a way to make a creative association. The more information you can gather about a person, the easier it will be for you to create a mental file for them. We also like to visually spell out their name in our minds as another memory trick.

When ending a conversation say, "It was so nice to meet you, Jennifer. I hope our paths cross again soon." This helps cement their name one last time before parting ways. If appropriate, ask for their business card and read it. Seeing their name in writing helps too.

So what do you do if you've tried all the memory tricks and simply forget the name of someone you have met before? You see them walking toward you with a great smile, hand extended. You've made eye contact, so you can't turn and walk away. Nor can you very well ask them for their card–you are supposed to know them already. In times like this, it is important to remain calm and not act awkward and apologetic. Do not beat yourself up, everyone forgets from time to time.

In this situation when you absolutely cannot remember their name, give them a warm genuine greeting, smile, extend your hand, reintroduce yourself and say something about when you last met, "Hi, it is so nice to see you again, I'm Francesca Apple and we met at the accounting seminar last month." They are likely to respond with something along the lines of, "oh yes, I remember you and I am John Taylor. How have you been?" Easy breezy, problem solved.

Unfortunately, sometimes the other person won't cooperate and volunteer their name in greeting you. In that case, your next sentence should be something along the lines of, "Would you please tell me your name again? It is right on the tip of my tongue." Try not to say that you forgot or don't remember their name because those phrases may make the other person feel badly. Once they provide their name, repeat it and immediately follow up with a memory of when you last met. This reinforces the point that you do remember them. Again, remember that everyone forgets every now and again. Just be marvelously well-mannered and reintroduce yourself often. You may very well be helping someone who has a memory lapse of their own!

Applying this in the real world

Q. Sometimes I find myself talking with someone when another person whose name I cannot remember comes up. What do I do?

A. Warmly greet them with a smile and a handshake. Ask them how they have been and then immediately do a half introduction. Say, "I'd like you to meet Mike Stone (the name of the person you were standing with)" as you turn your gaze to Mike and keep your gaze there on Mike. This will encourage the new person to also look at Mike and spur Mike to introduce himself. Follow up with additional information to help continue the conversation.

Q. Is it ok to ask for a business card to help you remember someone's name?

A. Yes, as long as you don't say that is why you are asking for it. In cases like this, it is ok to say a little white lie, "my contact list got messed up in my latest upgrade, may I please have your card again?" When they hand it over, look at it, then put it away.

Here's My Card:

BUSINESS CARD ETIQUETTE

Someone recently asked, "Does anyone use business cards anymore?" We were surprised–and pleased–with the amount of interest that resulted from this seemingly simple Facebook post. And the answers–from a varied peanut gallery that included both younger and more seasoned professionals in DC and across the country, those in public service in our military, Capitol Hill staffers and a diverse group of private sector employees–overwhelmingly said, YES.

◼

A few folks tried to argue that LinkedIn gives you all you need to know. While we love LinkedIn, it cannot replace the look, feel, and connection that comes from the ritual of exchanging business cards.

Aside from telling people that you work for a certain employer, business cards are part of your individual brand's communications package and they should clearly send the message that you are a professional and take your career seriously. There are a few simple steps you can take to make sure that those who receive your business card remember you and your personal brand for all the right reasons.

Make sure you have a **professional-looking business card**. Most of us are issued employer-approved business cards, so you have to take what you get. But if you are a budding entrepreneur and have your own cards, put some time and effort into selecting the proper paper stock, font, coloring, etc. so that it is a card that has a professional look and feel. By a professional look and feel, we don't mean stuffy or conservative. We have pink and green business cards ourselves and think them quite marvelous! What we mean is whether or not your card extends your personal brand as a professional in your line of work such that it will help you achieve success. If not, you should rethink your card's motif. You want your card to work for you, not against you.

Keep your cards **clean and crisp**. The easiest method for keeping your cards in tip-top shape is to put them in a case for protection. Don't forget that the card case itself reflects on your personal brand. Regularly replenish your card case and keep it in a convenient place on your person so that you aren't the person giving themselves a pat-down or frantically digging through their work bag searching for the card case when asked for your card.

When you hand out your card, present it with two hands, holding each side with your thumbs and index finger so that the writing is face-up to the recipient. You don't want to make them turn it over or turn it right-side-up to be able to read it. Make it easy for them to remember you.

When someone hands you their business card, you should accept it (ideally with two hands as described) and **pause to look at it**. This is a sign of respect, not a sign of weakness ("oh, darned, they are going to know I had to look at their name."). Take the time to burn that name into your brain to help you remember. Then put it away. Wait until later to jot down a few notes that will help you remember the person, the connection, and the conversation when you next run into them. You will look in control and at the top of your game. Writing on someone's card when you are still in their presence is considered rude.

Lastly, know that cards are usually exchanged at the **end of a conversation**, and are exchanged between people who are starting to develop a relationship. This helps prevent you from ambushing people you don't know, handing out your card like a flyer to a free concert. Nor should you ask someone with whom you have yet to have a conversation for their card. You need to establish some sort of concrete connection first.

Follow these tips, build your personal professional brand, and soon others will be asking for your business card.

Applying this in the real world

Q. What happens if I can't hand over my card with both hands?

A. On the occasions that one of your hands is occupied with a cocktail or a file or some other item (not your mobile phone, which should be put away when engaging in face-to-face conversations), simply hand over the card with one hand using the thumb and finger grip as described previously. Make sure the card is facing forward and upright toward the recipient, so they can easily read it.

Q. I have heard that junior professionals can't ask more senior people for their card. Is that true?

A. It has less to do with seniority that it does with concrete connections. Younger, more junior professionals can certainly ask to exchange cards with a more seasoned leader in the industry if you have had a conversation. You cannot just walk up to the VIP, say, "hi," and ask for their card and force yours in their hand. Don't be that person. They will likely hand theirs over and take yours, but you will be branded as a bit boorish and they will likely never take your call.

Don't Get Tangled Up in Telephone Technology Trouble

No doubt, technology has become an integral part of our lives. We need to use it for good, not bad. Whether we realize it or not, technology influences how we act and affects how others perceive us. The goal of this chapter is to help you avoid getting tangled up in tech trouble. The easiest way to do that is to remember how important it is to follow the rules of etiquette and maintain your personal brand across all the platforms on which you communicate. Too often people think it is okay to short-circuit manners and civility on tech devices because you aren't face-to-face and you are supposed to be casual and quick in your communications.

Wrong.

Focusing on manners and etiquette on tech devices is critical because there are so many opportunities for misunderstanding. The person you are communicating with can't get the full picture. Rarely can they hear your voice, understand your tone, see your body language, or easily tell when something is a joke.

It goes without saying, when you are face-to-face with someone, put all technology down. Focus on the person in front of you and make them your priority, not the person on the other end of your device. When you interrupt a face-to-face conversation to take a call or send a text, you send the clear signal to the person standing right in front of you that they are not a priority to you. This is bad in both business and life.

When you are speaking on the phone, smile. You sound more pleasant when you do. Speak clearly, loudly, and slowly so that the other person does not have to strain to hear or understand you. It's important to focus on the person you are speaking with, even when they can't see you. This means that you shouldn't multitask while sitting at your desk on a conference call. If you think you are being responsive with an "um" "yeah" "uh-huh", you aren't.

Speaking of phones, watch out for overuse of speakerphones. Don't be that person who always uses speakerphone–particularly in an open office. When you do, you disrupt the quiet working environment of your peers. They aren't at all interested in listening to a conference call they weren't invited to in the first place. They have their own work to do. And please don't be that person who walks around with your mobile device on speakerphone. It just bugs everyone—and we mean literally, everyone—who you walk by.

When using a mobile phone, remember that you don't need to yell into it for the other person to hear you. Technology has advanced so there is no need to be "yellular". If you are out in public and take a call, go off to the side (away from others) and cup your hand over your mouth so passersby don't have to suffer through listening to half a phone conversation (which many find quite irritating). Additionally, a ringtone you find nifty may irritate others (and may be inappropriate during working hours), so watch the volume. Consider putting your phone on vibrate.

While millennials may be comfortable using technology while in the presence of others, many in the business world find it rude when you text others in front of them. Focus on the person you are with, not the person on the other end of your electronic device.

In addition to phone tech etiquette, when sending emails, remember to never send one when angry. Wait for your cooler head to prevail. Never write something you don't want others to read. Assume if you are writing about someone, they will somehow see that email. It is best to remember that business emails are business and should maintain a level of business formality. Use salutations, watch your grammar, check your spelling, and close with a signature. If you find yourself in a lengthy email exchange with someone, consider picking up the phone to talk or walking down the hall to talk face-to-face. Many misunderstandings can be avoided as you confirm facts on a live call or in person. Always do your best to answer business emails within 24 hours.

Applying this in the real world

Q. Is it ok for me to add people on blind copy when I send emails?

A. We strongly advise against that unless it is standard practice in the company. Oftentimes the person you put on blind copy ends up hitting reply-all and their presence on the email chain is revealed.

Q. I like to use speakerphone so that I can take notes from the call. Why can't I?

A. You can use speakerphone but do so politely. Close the door so you don't bother others or use headphones. Let the person on the other end know they are on speakerphone. This timely disclosure avoids them saying something sensitive or inappropriate to an unknown audience.

Savvy Social Media

It seems like every week brings us a new, unfortunate example of someone doing something wrong on social media–and paying the price. Sometimes that price is the loss of their job, even if their social media usage had nothing to do with their job. While more and more people feel comfortable putting their opinions, their activities, and their thoughts on display, more and more people also feel comfortable (and entitled) to pass judgment online too. There seems to be no end to the mob mentality of the public shaming of others. Sometimes social media isn't all that "social"—indeed it can be downright snarky[27]. Resultantly, it is important to remember that once you post, tweet, or otherwise put something out on social media sites, you cannot take it back and you *will* be judged.

Don't rely on your privacy settings to protect you. There is no such thing as privacy when it comes to the social media use of digital technology. Review your employer's social media policy so you know the rules you are required to follow if you want to keep your job.

Before you post or tweet something, ask yourself: Is it true? Is it necessary? Is it kind? If you answer "no" to any of those questions, rethink your need to put it out there in the first place. Just because you have an opinion on a subject doesn't mean it is always necessary to share that opinion with the world. Likewise, going on a rant and swearing up a storm is rarely productive. Think about it. When was the last time someone's profanity-laced rant changed your mind on a particular subject? The only thing it is likely to change is someone's once favorable view of you. You go down a definite peg or two when you lose self-control and self-respect with such a rant and act cruel or snarky towards others.

It is easy to forget that there is a live human being on the other end of others' social media accounts. If you wouldn't say something to a person's face while standing next to your employer, parent, or child, you should not want to say it on social media–where it lives forever. Your personal brand should be consistent across all social media platforms and be consistent with who you are in the physical, real world. You can't be one person online and a completely different person in person. When you are, you lose credibility.

Let positivity be part of your brand. As such, do not complain about your work, your boss, your clients, your customers, or your colleagues on social media sites. Unless it is part of your job, you should not be on social media sites during work hours (minus breaks and lunch).

Don't post videos or tag photos of others without their permission. Ask when taking the photo. Ask parents before posting pictures of their children. It doesn't matter if "everyone else does it". Trust us, if you ask, most parents will be grateful and appreciative. Never tag unflattering photos of others; it just isn't a kind thing to do. And when someone asks you to delete a photo or untag them, do it.

In sum, please watch the grammar, keep it upbeat, and keep it safe. Pure and simple.

As a last note on the topic, remember to take a tech time out often and engage others face-to-face. It is very satisfying engaging with a live person over a cup of coffee or tea or a glass of wine (with your cell phone tucked away). That is the real way to be social in this social-media-driven world.

Applying this in the real world

Q. I hosted a holiday party and now want to post pictures on my Facebook page. Do I have to ask everyone in all the photos for their permission?

A. Was it a work or social party? How many photos are you posting? Use discretion when it is a work event. Less is more and when in doubt, don't. If it was more of a social party, in the likely event that everyone you are "friends" with on Facebook was not invited to the party (even if they live close by), you may want to self-edit your photos so that you only post a few as opposed to a whole album. Many people find it quite isolating and depressing to see the fun their friends partook in that didn't include them. Find a few flattering photos of your guests at the party and quickly let them know you want to post photos and ask if they mind if you tag them. Better yet, next time, ask just before you take the photo. A quick, "I am going to share the good photos on Facebook if you don't mind" will do.

Q. My Facebook account is personal. Why do I have to worry about work repercussions when I post?

A. You only need to look at the new stories popping up every day where someone loses their job because of what they posted, tweeted, or commented on–even when they were not at work or it had nothing to do with work. Most private employers have social media policies. You should read them. Your employer wants you to reflect well on the company. With today's social networks, your off-hours, off-color behavior can get you in trouble. If it isn't true, kind, or necessary, ask yourself why you are posting, tweeting, or commenting in the first place.

20

Not Another
Business Meeting

If you are reading this book, you are probably in the professional world and go to meetings–far too many meetings. Most of us find meetings dreadful because some aren't pleasant or particularly productive. Often the culprit is a lack of basic manners in those meetings. Whether you run a meeting or attend a meeting, there are business etiquette steps you should take to make the meeting more productive and pleasant for everyone.

If you are running a meeting, remember, **agendas are your friend**. Send one out far enough in advance so that others have an opportunity to come prepared for your meeting.

Be early for your meetings. You should greet those attending your meeting. They are your guests, so to speak. This also gives you time to network before the meeting and a lot goes on at the little "meeting before the meeting". This is a great opportunity to deepen relationships or casually strategize on work projects.

Being early for your meetings also helps you start your meeting on time. It is important to respect others' schedules and when you start and conclude your meeting on time, you do just that.

The person who runs the meeting is the traffic cop of the meeting, **keeping it on topic and on time**. That means you need to make sure the meeting follows the agenda. If people bring up items not on the agenda, you need to politely close down that conversation and suggest scheduling another meeting or adding it to next week's agenda. Additionally, when people take too much time talking about a subject that is on the agenda, you need to manage that discussion as well. You cannot let those deep-dives knock you off schedule.

Being a traffic cop also means regulating what people say and how they behave in your meetings. Do not let someone belittle, yell, swear at, cut-off, dismiss, or condescend another colleague. When you let that type of behavior go unchecked, you send the clear message that you condone that behavior. Resultantly, your meetings will suffer because people will dread going if they know they may be the subject of someone else's tirade. They will start to check-out. Then your meetings aren't as productive as they should be. As the one running the meetings, it is incumbent on you to expect attendees to showcase good manners.

If you are the one attending the meeting, there are things you can do to look professional and well-mannered and help encourage a more productive and pleasant meeting.

Arrive a bit early. This enables you to choose your seat and get settled. Each seat has with it a corresponding piece of the conference table. You want to use all the real estate assigned to your seat. Oftentimes, people signal they are insecure or unsure of themselves by literally folding themselves up and taking up as little space as possible. Do not be that person. Use your body language to signal you are confident, engaged, and have something to contribute. This means sitting up straight, having organized materials, and using all the real estate that is assigned to your seat. On the flip side, don't be that person who overspreads and takes up more space than is properly assigned. That too signals you are insecure (as well as aggressive).

Be prepared for all meetings so that you can meaningfully contribute. But recognize that meetings are not monologues where you get to lecture your colleagues. They are dialogues where you work together to achieve a common goal. And when a decision has been made by the higher-ups, don't waste everyone else's time by complaining about or explaining why your boss is wrong or, alternatively, sulk at the end of the conference table. The. Decision. Has. Been. Made. Recognize your place in the hierarchy. Recognize some decisions are not yours to make. Rather, your job at that point is to execute on the plan.

Show respect to your colleagues by **paying attention** when they speak. Give them eye contact, nod when you are listening, don't interrupt them, and don't look at your electronic devices. You think no one sees you texting on your mobile phone under the table–they all see you. If you are taking notes on your laptop, it's okay provided you send the clear signal that you are on the device in furtherance of the meeting. You can do this by not surfing the Internet or checking and answering emails during the meeting. If you are looking up something, say it is for the meeting. "Susie, do you want me to look up the dates of that conference?" Easy, breezy.

Applying this in the real world

Q. I have a staffer who likes to get granular in their discussion and my meetings often run over. What can I do?

A. If someone is talking about an agenda item but is going down a rabbit hole in terms of substance, you need to quickly get your meeting back on track. Smile and make eye contact while saying, "These are good points but for this meeting, we just need to decide X. If we need to talk further, and it looks like we might need to do so, let's find another time to do a deeper dive. I don't want this meeting to run over. I will send a calendar invite after this meeting." Everyone else will appreciate you respecting their schedules. However, if this happens regularly, you may want to consider putting less items on your meeting agenda which would let you allocate more time to each subject or meet separately with that particular staffer who may need more guidance, direction, or feedback to complete their projects.

Q. Someone recently brought up an important subject at a meeting– it wasn't on the agenda. I wasn't prepared. What could I have done? I wasn't running the meeting, so I didn't know what to do.

A. It is hard when you aren't running the meeting. If you felt comfortable, you could have suggested to the one running the meeting, "I agree with (name the person who raised the issue) that this is an important subject. And I have some information to contribute but don't have it all here with me. Could we possibly put it on next week's meeting agenda or schedule a separate meeting?" This sends the polite signal that this is important and even though it wasn't on the agenda, you are a team player and want to contribute.

21

Common Areas—the Place to Use Common Sense:

RESPECTING THE TIME AND SPACE OF OTHERS

Most work places have common items and places that are shared by all employees. For example, it is common to have a break room with tables, a microwave, coffee pots, water, and a refrigerator. Your company is gracious enough to provide these items to add some convenience to your break and lunch times, so it is important for everyone to clean up after themselves.

When you use something, clean it after your use so that it is cleaner than you found it. This means taking a damp sponge or a Clorox wipe and wiping down the table even if you don't think you spilled anything. Wash, dry, and put away all utensils and plates and glassware you use. Do not be the person who leaves coffee mugs, spoons, and the like in the sink for someone else (usually more junior) to clean. That is not a nice thing to do. It does not help your personal brand either.

If your organization has a dishwasher—lucky you! Your colleagues will think highly of you if you unload it once in a while too.

Keep track of the food and drink that you bring into the common areas. Clearly label your products as yours and including a date on it will help you keep track of items that may soon expire. It takes group effort to keep the fridge clean—far too often people put items in the fridge and never take them out again. We have all been there. We pack our lunch but then decide to go out instead. You can do your part by checking the fridge on a weekly basis to make sure your items haven't expired or been otherwise abandoned.

And it goes without saying, only use your items or items that are clearly marked common like creamer, coconut milk, honey, or sugar.

The principle of cleaning up after yourself also applies to all common equipment. Most of us have to share color printers and photocopiers. If you use the last piece of paper in the tray, refill it. If you cause a paper jam, fix it. Do not leave your messes for others to deal with.

We also want to take the opportunity here to talk about respecting the space of others. As more and more organizations utilize open-area work concepts, it is important to regulate your behavior so that you aren't a distraction to your colleagues. We all make noise and need to be mindful of that. Don't snap your gum. It may sound neat to you, but it is annoying to others. If you have long nails, please watch your typing, making sure you type with the pad of your finger instead of the long nail that results in loud clicking. Don't be a pounder when you type either. It is distracting to others. Be mindful of colleagues trying to concentrate next to you if you are on a phone call or are talking to a small group of colleagues. Take your conversations, if possible, elsewhere. Make your call in a conference room or a phone call room. Take extended conversations to a conference room or the break room. A little courtesy makes everyone's day more productive and pleasant.

Being respectful of colleagues in open-work areas also means not touching colleagues' items despite them being out in the open. It means not looking over their shoulder at their work product. It means approaching them from the front or the side–so they see you coming– instead of ambushing them from behind. Think of all the things your colleagues do that annoy you and try not to do them to others.

Applying this in the real world

Q. I do my part, but there are a few colleagues of mine who never clean up after themselves and leave their junk in the sink for others to clean. What can we do?

A. How rude of them to think that they can just leave their things in the sink for others to clean. You could ask the office manager to remind everyone of the break room policy and post it so that everyone is aware of what the rules are. If your office is smaller and that isn't an option, you could say to them, "Would you please clean up after yourself so that we don't have to do it for you?" We heard of one office–that was fairly small–giving personalized mugs to everyone so that it was abundantly clear who was making the mess and who wasn't.

Q. I work with a thief. Someone keeps taking my cans of La Croix passion fruit soda water. What should I do?

A. Take a quick stroll around the office, do you see someone drinking your brand? If so, you could go up, smile, and politely ask if they took that from the break room refrigerator. If they say, "yes", you then should respond by saying with a smile, "you probably didn't realize but I actually bought those sodas for me to drink." They will likely apologize, which you should graciously accept. But what if you don't see the perpetrator? While you may want to sit and wait, so you can catch the person red-handed, that isn't the most productive use of your time. You could clearly mark each can (instead of the 12-pack box) with your initials so that they would have a hard time drinking out of the can with your initials on it. Or you may want to bring in a smaller cooler and keep a few cans in it under your desk. They will have a harder time stealing your water and it will be easier for you to get to.

Top-Drawer
Thank You Notes

"The letter you write, whether you realize it or not, is always a mirror which reflects your appearance, taste and character."—EMILY POST

In business, there are many instances when a thank you note is in order. Someone might take you to lunch or dinner. Or send you a gift, flowers for your birthday, or the latest industry book, or someone invited you to be their guest to a charity event. When in doubt, why NOT thank them? Thanking someone for a gift or an act of kindness is something nice you can do, pure and simple. Yes, you should thank them in person, but you should also follow up with a written thank you.

Email thank you notes are perfectly acceptable, and many people say thank you this way. But because so many people say thank you this way, it is a bit routine. A handwritten note takes you from routine to remarkable in five short minutes.

Thank-you notes are to be mailed within the week. The sooner you do it, the less likely you are to forget. Oftentimes, despite the best intentions, it is hard to get that note written and out the door because you don't have stamps or stationery, or you don't know the mailing address. To help set you up for success, be prepared. Keep a supply of stamps and stationery at your desk.

We address and stamp the envelope before we head out making it much more likely that we will actually write three or four lines of appreciation when we get back. Then the only thing left to do is to seal the envelope and walk it to the mailbox.

But wait, we aren't done! We need to explain *how* to write a proper thank you note. Writing a marvelously well-mannered thank you note is an art form, not a science, but here are some basic principles that should be included in every single one:

- ✓ An enthusiastic opening
- ✓ Explicit "Thank you" for the gift/nicety
- ✓ Explain how you are going to use what they gave you or how much you appreciated their kindness
- ✓ A second, "Thank you"
- ✓ A closing

Writing thank you notes is a wonderful habit to develop and handwritten notes are a sure way to immediately stand out and be remembered.

Applying this in the real world

Q. My company doesn't offer free stationery. Do I still need to write handwritten thank you notes?

A. You don't have to send handwritten thank you notes, but we encourage you to do so from a personal branding perspective. You don't have to spend oodles of money on stationery. There is much to choose from at all price points. We encourage you to pick something that will reflect your personal brand and that is professional. Remember, what you write on, as well as what you write, is a reflection of you.

Q. I am pretty casual when I thank friends–usually I just text or shoot a quick email. What type of closing should I use when writing thank you notes in business?

A. Thank you notes should end on a good note. "Sincerely" or "Warm Regards" are entirely appropriate closings to use in a business setting.

PART III

DINING SKILLS.

There will be many times in business when you are invited to break bread with your boss, colleagues, clients, or customers. But make no mistake, don't view this meal as merely an opportunity to eat. If it involves business, it is another opportunity to showcase your professionalism. Your dining companions will watch what you order, how you eat, how you treat the wait-staff, how you engage in delightful chit-chat, and how you handle any mishaps. They do this to get insight into your character. But there is no reason to be nervous. There are ample opportunities for you to practice until you have it down pat. The following chapters will explain everything you need to know to dine successfully. When you know what to do and how to do it, you will gain a quiet confidence at the dining table that will add to your professional brand. You will no longer need to worry about yourself. Instead, you will be able to focus on those you are dining with and the business agenda at hand. How marvelous!

23

Run of Show:

PLACE SETTING

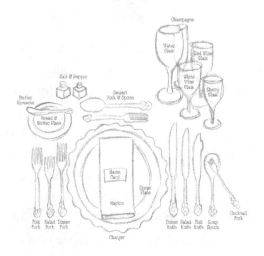

In show business, the term "run of show" explains how an event on a stage is going to unfold. It tells those working the event what they need to know and what they need to do to pull off a successfully executed event. It details what is going to happen when, and resultantly what everyone needs to do when. It is very comforting knowing the run of show before an event. Likewise, the place setting tells diners the "run of show" for the meal. The table is set in such a way that it explains how many courses there will be and what to do when. When we know how to read the most elaborate of place settings, all other meals are a cakewalk. You will confidently dine no matter how formal the occasion. You won't have to worry about what fork to use when, or why there are utensils above the plate.

The general rule is that forks are on the left and knives and spoons are on the right. To help you remember, think F-O-R-K is four letters just like the word "left". K-N-I-F-E and S-P-O-O-N each have five letters just like the word "right". The table is set so that the utensils you will use first are placed on the outer edges and you work your way in. This makes sense because it would be awkward if you tried to pick up utensils closest to the plate without disturbing the remaining utensils.

One exception to the general rule stated above is when the table is pre-set for the dessert course. The fork and spoon are placed above the plate just like the illustration. The other exception to the general rule is the small cocktail fork. Its tines are placed in the bowl of the soupspoon, as illustrated above.

When your table is elaborately set, like the illustration, it tells us that we are having six courses–starting with a seafood cocktail course, followed by a soup course, a fish course, a salad course, a main course, and, lastly, dessert.

The out-to-in rule applies to stemware as well. The illustration lets us know that the host has paired our courses with drinks, starting with the sherry and working in. Because there are both white and red glasses we know that the main course is going to be a meat of some kind–to pair with the red wine. The white wine goes with the fish course.

Keep in mind that wine pairings have gotten increasingly bold and flexible over the years. For example, there are delightfully light reds that go well with fish.

If the wait-staff asks you to choose white or red, you get to choose what you drink with your course. This illustration also tells us that there is going to be a champagne toast at the end of the evening as the champagne flute is one of the last glasses set. The water goblet is always on the inside and all of the other glasses to its right.

The bread plate is on the left side of the place setting. Sometimes people have a hard time remembering this, particularly when the table is set so tight that the place settings are practically touching the ones next to them. Here is an illustration to help you remember that bread is on the left and drinks are on the right. You can replicate this inconspicuously with your hands in your lap when you are out:

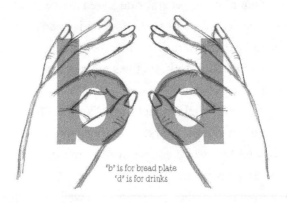

'b' is for bread plate
'd' is for drinks

The bread plate sometimes has a butter spreader on it, like the illustration. The communal butter plate should have its own butter knife for you to transfer the butter to your plate. If it does not, use your butter spreader to take the butter and place it on your bread plate. *Never put it directly on the bread.*

Applying this in the real world

Q. I recently went to a dinner party and there weren't as many courses as this illustration. I am so confused–what do I do?

A. Once you know how to maneuver your way around a dining table that is elaborately set, you will know how to handle less formal affairs. The same rules apply no matter how many courses are served at a meal. Start out-to-in with your utensils. When in doubt, follow your host's lead. Presumably they have set the table and know what utensils are to be used when. As you wait for the host to pick up their utensils, take a sip of water, or engage in a conversation with someone seated next to you. You need not be the first one to pick up your utensils.

Q. Someone used my bread plate recently. I ended up not eating any bread but that is my favorite food. What should I have done?

A. You behaved perfectly appropriate. The number one rule is to never point out another person's mistake. We never call attention to someone else's faux pas–that is not nice. You were right not to say, "hey, stop using my plate!" You were also right in not then stealing the bread plate of the person to your right. Two wrongs don't make a right. You basically had two options. You could have taken a roll and placed it on the rim of your main plate. Or you could have refrained from any bread.

Don't Wave the White Flag Yet:

LEARN NAPKIN ETIQUETTE

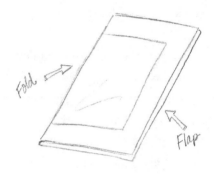

The rules of napkin etiquette are easy and straightforward.

When the host picks up their napkin, it signals that the meal is starting and you should do the same. If there is no "host" at the table, place the napkin on your lap immediately after you take your seat. If you are the host, don't forget to put your napkin on your lap—others are waiting for you.

Note, while grace is not said at a business meal, if you are otherwise dining with people who are known to say grace before they eat, refrain from picking up the napkin until after grace is said.

If you are seated at a table waiting for your guest, you should wait for your guest to be seated before removing the napkin from your place setting. This enables your dining companion to see a pristine, completely set table.

Luncheon napkins are smaller than normal formal dinner napkins. The traditional luncheon napkin is 14-16 inches and is to be open fully and placed on your lap. The formal dinner napkin is 22-26 inches and is not to be open fully. Open it so that it is folded in half and place it on your lap with the fold part closest to your waist and the side with the two flaps closest to your knees.

To properly use the napkin, bring it up to your mouth to blot your lips–do not wipe or smear. To clean your fingers gently open the flaps and wipe them on the *inside* of the napkin. This helps keep your clothes free from food and grease. A napkin is used only to keep your mouth and hands clean. When using a tea or luncheon napkin take extra care to eat slowly and neatly because if you have to use your napkin it is fully open and has no inside flaps to use. Napkins are not used to wipe your face of sweat, nor should they be used as a handkerchief. Napkins should not be used to store or hide inedible pieces of food.

When excusing yourself mid-meal and planning to return to the table, loosely gather your napkin and lay it across the seat of your chair. It does not go on the table, on the arm of the chair, or the back of the chair. It belongs on the seat. This signals to wait-staff and others in the know that you will be returning so that they don't clear your plate.

Please note that some restaurants have instructed their wait-staff to pick up your napkin from the seat of your chair and refold your gently-used napkin and place it on the table when you have excused yourself mid-meal. This is incorrect, but there isn't much you can do about it. We don't advise lecturing staff on the finer points of napkin etiquette. They are only doing what they have been told to do by their superiors. While we are certain well-meaning restaurant management is asking their staff to do this as a way of providing superior service and enhanced customer attention, the unfortunate result is that it confuses patrons into thinking they should put their used napkin on the table when they are excusing themselves mid-meal. And as we just explained, that is incorrect.

The only time a used napkin goes back on the table is when you are done with your meal. When you are done eating, gently gather your napkin and place it to the left of the plate or if the plate has been cleared, placed in the spot where the main course plate used to be. You should not be the first to put your napkin on the table when you are the guest. At the end of the meal, it is the duty of the host to signal–by placing their napkin on the table–that the meal has concluded. Once that is done, you loosely gather your napkin and place it to the left of your place setting or in front of you if your plate has been removed. Do not refold it.

Applying this in the real world

Q. Where does the napkin ring go after you remove the napkin?

A. Napkin rings are used at casual meals inside the home. Napkin rings enabled family members to keep and reuse their own gently used napkin for multiple meals. But more and more restaurants are utilizing pretty napkin rings as a way to enhance the beauty of their tablescape. A napkin ring is placed to the left of your plate above the forks once you remove it from the napkin. It does not belong to the right of your plate where there is stemware and it can cause accidents.

Q. What do I do if I have to sneeze and I don't have time to excuse myself from the table or have a tissue on me?

A. This scenario is exactly why you should always have a tissue or a handkerchief handy. But if you don't have one and you feel a massive sneeze coming–one that really does require a tissue– turn away from the table, into your shoulder and use your napkin as a shield. Once the sneeze has passed, excuse yourself from the table and take the napkin with you. Leave it in the bathroom and freshen up. Napkins should not be used as handkerchiefs but if it is the only thing available in an emergency, common sense should prevail–use it. Then ask for a new napkin.

Rounding Out the Meal:

SOUPS, SALAD, AND BREAD

Knowing your way around your place setting is a must for dining etiquette. Sometimes people overlook the to-dos associated with soups, salads, and bread because they aren't the star attractions. But these foods often play supporting roles in a meal. We want to make sure you know about them so that you are marvelously well-mannered throughout the entire meal–not just the main event.

Soup is a course in itself. Soups are served either in a soup plate (a low shallow bowl on top of a flat plate that serves as a saucer of sorts) or a soup bowl (a bowl with higher sides atop a smaller saucer). Soup can be served as the first course or, at more formal occasions, served after a seafood cocktail or fruit cocktail first course. If the table is pre-set, you will find the soupspoon on the right side of the place setting, to the right of the knives. Otherwise, wait-staff will bring your soupspoon when they bring the soup. Your dominant hand's index finger and middle finger are used to hold the soupspoon steady. Imagine the spoon is a pencil and hold it accordingly, with your thumb resting gently on the top of the handle. Do not grip the soupspoon with your fist.

Wait for your soup to cool before taking a spoonful. Do not blow on it–that shows a lack of patience.

"Like a ship sailing out to sea,
I spoon my soup away from me." — UNKNOWN

Spoon the soup away from you. Gently slide the bottom of the soupspoon on the lip of the soup plate or soup bowl to wipe off any drips. (Stews and chowders are the exception and are spooned towards you). Bring the soupspoon up to your mouth and gently sip from the side when eating a clear broth soup. If you are eating a soup filled with vegetables and meat, you put the soupspoon in your mouth, tip first. If the soup is served in a soup plate, the soupspoon is placed in the soup plate at 10:20 when you are resting and when you are finished with your course. In contrast, if the soup is served in a soup bowl, the soupspoon is placed on the saucer that is *under* the soup bowl when resting between sips of soup and when finished.

There is a lot of flexibility when it comes to serving **salads**. In the United States, the salad course is typically served before the main course. While more common outside the United States, keep in mind that a salad course may be served after the main course. The salad fork's placement will tell you. If the salad is served before the main course, the salad fork will be to the left of the main course fork. If the salad is served after the main course, the salad fork will be found to the right of the main course fork. The salad fork is easily identified as the slightly shorter and smaller one when compared to the main course fork. If there is no fork at your place setting, the wait-staff will bring out utensils for you to use as needed.

Ideally, you won't need a knife to eat a salad because the lettuce and other ingredients will be precut before being plated. *Don't shove large bites into your mouth.* If you need to cut the salad, do so one bite at a time. Use the knife that is paired with your salad fork. It will be located on the right side of the place setting next to the main course knife. If the salad is served before the main course, the salad knife (slightly smaller than the main course knife) will be to the right of the main course knife. If the salad is served after the main course, the salad knife will be found to the left of the main course knife. If one is not provided, you have two options: (1) request a knife from the wait-staff or (2) use the knife for the next course and ask for a new knife for the next course.

Salad may also be served with the main meal. When it is, you will not be provided a separate salad fork and knife. You will use the utensils intended for the main course. The salad may be plated on the main dish plate or may be served on a separate, small salad plate that is located to the left of your main course plate.

Regardless of how the salad is served, when you are done with the course, place both your fork and knife on the plate at the 10:20 location. The fork tines will be up or down depending on if you are eating American (up) or Continental (down) style. If you ate the salad and did not need to use the knife that was provided for the course, still pick it up and place it on the plate with the fork in the "finished" position. (See Chapter 26 on utensil placement).

The **bread plate** is quite small and is found to the left of your place setting, above the forks. Each bread plate should have a butter spreader placed across the top of it, with the blade to the left and the handle on the right. Alternatively, you may find the butter spreader placed vertically on the right side of the plate. Bread or a roll may already be on the plate, along with a pad of butter. Or more likely, a breadbasket will be passed around followed by a communal plate of butter. Take one piece of bread or one roll at a time. The communal butter plate should have with it a butter knife. If so, use it to transfer the butter onto your bread plate. *Never take butter from the communal butter plate and put the butter directly on the bread.* The butter goes on your bread plate. If there is no communal butter knife, use your butter spreader. If there is no butter spreader, then use one of the knives from your place setting and then rest that knife across your bread plate until future use.

To eat the bread, break it with your fingers. Bread or rolls are never cut. Holding the roll or bread close to the plate, break off one bite-sized piece, butter it if you wish, then eat. Repeat as necessary. Never break the roll into pieces all at once. Never butter the entire roll or piece of bread at one time. Break and butter one piece at a time. Take your time–do not gobble your bread.

Applying this in the real world

Q. I have a hard time eating cherry tomatoes in my salad.

A. When you are out at an important business meal, we recommend avoiding difficult to eat foods–that includes the delicious cherry tomato. It just isn't worth the risk of trying to bite or cut into a cherry tomato. You are at a business meal for a purpose other than eating.

Q. Can I use my bread as a pusher to get food on my fork? Can I use it to sop up gravy?

A. Using bread as a utensil is not proper dining etiquette so don't do it at formal dining occasions. In formal dining, the knife is used to push food against the fork. In informal dining, the knife or a piece of bread is used as the pusher. Sopping up the extra gravy is done with a piece of bread on the end of the fork. Do not use your hands.

Silverware Success

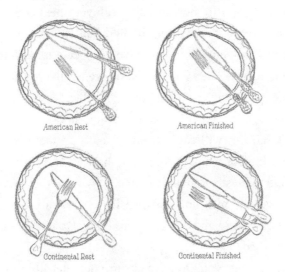

American Rest

American Finished

Continental Rest

Continental Finished

The proper use of silverware is a sure sign of a well-mannered diner. One does not touch the silverware until the food has arrived. This means no rearranging, touching, or absent-mindedly moving utensils without a reason for doing so. If you are moving your knife to keep it from falling, that's good. If you are moving it because you are fidgety, that's bad. As explained in Chapter 23, silverware is used from out to in, meaning that the silverware farthest from the plate is used first, then you would work your way inward using the next set of silverware for the next course, and so on.

When you do pick up your silverware to use it, do not make gestures with them. Safety first. If you have ever been seated next to someone gesturing wildly with their knife as they tell a funny story, you know what we are talking about. Once you pick up and use a utensil, it rests on the plate–never back on the table or the tablecloth. Some restaurants prefer that you reuse your utensils from course to course. If that is the case, you may place your utensils on the bread plate or politely ask for new utensils with your next course.

If you drop your utensil on the floor, quietly get the wait-staff's attention and let them know you have dropped a utensil and politely request a new one. They will pick it up–generally you should not do so because dirty utensils do not go on the table. However, you should pick up a dropped utensil if it is in the wait-staff's path or otherwise is a safety hazard (will cause tripping, etc.). In that case, pick it up and keep it in your hand, politely call the wait-staff over and hand it to them and request another clean one.

When you do pick up your utensils to start eating, remember to keep your elbows in and close to your body. Do not spread them out to cut your food.

When you cut your food, pick up your utensils (your knife in your dominant hand and your fork in your non-dominant hand) and curl your three fingers around each handle and secure your grip with your thumb. Your dominant hand's index finger should lay on the joint of the knife (where the blade and handle meet) while your other index finger should rest on the back of the fork right below the tines. The fork tines are facing down. Resting your index fingers on these spots will give you the control to easily and properly cut your food. This grip ensures you do not hold your utensils like a Neanderthal wielding a weapon or a cellist playing a musical piece. Cut one piece of food at time, regardless of the style of eating you choose. What you do after you cut the food will depend on that style of eating.

There are two styles of eating in the United States: American and Continental (also called European, but for our purposes, we will refer to it as Continental). Some enjoy eating using the American Style because it easier to learn and automatically slows down one's eating (as utensils change hands) while others prefer to use Continental because it is efficient and quiet (no clanging of utensils on the plate), not to mention it looks quite cosmopolitan. Both are appropriate and considered well-mannered. Choose one style and stick with it throughout your meal–from course to course. Otherwise you look a bit erratic.

When eating American style, start off holding your fork in your non-dominant hand, and your knife in your dominant hand. After you cut one piece of food, place your knife across the upper part of the plate with the blade toward the top center of your plate and the handle hanging off the right side and switch your fork to your dominant hand and eat, holding your fork like a pencil with the tines up and your thumb resting on the top of the handle. This is often referred to the "zig-zag" way of eating because you switch your utensils from one hand to the other to eat. Your free hand rests in your lap. When delivering the food to your mouth remember to sit up straight–the food comes up to your mouth. Your mouth does not come down to your food.

When you are at "rest"–not eating–you place your fork and knife on the plate parallel to each other but with some space in between. The knife lays across the top (think of the knife near 1:00 if the plate is the face of a clock) while the fork is in the center of the plate (near 4:00). One hand may rest in your lap while your other hand's wrist rests on the edge of the table. Avoid putting both hands in your lap. When you are "finished" with your meal place your fork and knife at 10:20 with the tops at the 10 o'clock hour location and the handles at the 20-minute location. The knife blade faces in toward the center of the plate and the fork tines are up.

When you eat Continental style, your utensils remain in the same hands–they never switch off. The fork starts and remains in your non-dominant hand. When you are done cutting your piece of food, keep hold of the knife but lift your hand with the fork up to your mouth and rotate your wrist to deliver the food into your mouth. The tines of your fork remain down throughout this process. Resultantly, the food is packaged on the back of your fork. Your knife acts as the "pusher" and it collects small samples of the food on the plate (meat is the anchor, then the veggies and other sides are added) and pushes the food onto the back of the fork creating a small package for you to eat.

If you normally have trouble eating slowly, you need to be doubly mindful when eating Continental style because there is no natural break in eating like with the American style. The "rest" position in Continental style is when the knife and fork are placed down creating a little "X" on the plate with the tines of the fork down and over the knife blade, which is facing in. Hands do not go in the lap when eating Continental style. When not holding utensils, the wrists are to rest on the edge of the table. The "finished" position is 10:20 but the tines of the fork are down.

Eating either way is being marvelously well-mannered–as long as you also sit up straight, eat quietly, and chew with your mouth closed. And remember, elbows off the table!

Applying this in the real world

Q. I find it uncomfortable holding the knife and fork as you describe when I am cutting. I like a firm grip–what is the harm?

A. The harm is that you look ill-mannered when you hold utensils improperly and table manners are viewed by many as a proxy for being well-mannered in general. One does not need an exceedingly strong grip to simply cut meat at the dining table. Your meat doesn't need to be attacked, so don't hold your utensils like weapons. Gently hold the utensils as described and practice cutting at home–in private–and it will soon become second nature.

Q. I like to eat Continental style, but I have a hard time eating rice and peas. What can I do?

A. When eating Continental style, it is important to create a small package of food on the back of the fork. Your meat is your anchor food–spear that first then use the blade of the knife to push (and mush) peas and rice onto the meat then bring your fork up to your mouth as you rotate your wrist (the fork tines will remain down) and eat. If you know what is being served, you can always decide at the beginning of the meal to eat American style. It is easier to eat peas and rice with the fork tines up.

27

What's Yours is Mine:

COMMUNAL ITEMS

There are a variety of items on the table that are to be shared with your dining companions: salt and pepper shakers, salad dressing, condiments, breadbasket, butter plate, coffee pot, cream, sugar, etc. Unsurprisingly, there are some rules of the road when it comes to sharing these items.

If there is a communal item in front of you, pick it up and pass it around, even if you don't want to use it. It is your job to make sure others have easy access to it. Don't wait for someone to ask for it, except when it comes to salt and pepper. More on that exception later.

If it is at all possible, please pass items to the right. When all items are passed in the same direction, traffic jams are avoided. However, if someone already started passing something to the left, go with the flow. Don't fall on your sword merely to follow the rule of passing to the right.

Whenever possible, place the item being passed directly on the table (as opposed to directly into someone else's hands) with the handles pointed toward the person who is going to next use the item. When you hand something off this way, spills and mishaps are avoided.

Please do not "shortstop" at the table. Shortstopping occurs when someone asks for something to be passed to them (for example, the breadbasket) and the person who begins to pass the requested item, or others along the way, take or use the requested item on its way around the table. That is bad form. If someone asks you for the breadbasket, do not take a roll for yourself before you send the basket on its journey around the table. And if you are one of the people passing the breadbasket along the route, you should not take a roll as you pass it along. This is not nice. Do not do it. It is considered rude. Wait until it reaches its intended location and then ask for the item back.

> *"Give neither counsel nor salt till you are asked for it."*
> – ITALIAN PROVERB

We are not big salt people. In fact, the only thing we add salt to is a margarita–yum! But we can still offer some sound advice when it comes to salt and pepper. When you want the salt, and it is not within easy reach, politely ask someone to, "please, pass the salt." Before you utter those words though, remember that you should taste the food to see if needs the seasoning.

If you are the one passing the salt, also pass the pepper. They are a pair. They go together!

When passing salt and pepper, place them on the table next to the person requesting the seasoning. Do not hand them directly to the other person.

Some establishments set the table so that everyone has, or every two people have, individual salt and pepper pairings. In those cases, use what is within easy reach and your dining companions will do the same.

The exception to the rule of keeping salt and pepper together is if the salt is in a salt cellar–a small dish placed on the table to house the salt. In that case, when someone asks for the salt, you only pass the salt cellar. There are a few additional rules for their use as well.

Most salt cellars come with tiny spoons which you use to place the salt on your food or plate. But if there is no spoon, use the tip of a clean knife to take some salt from the communal salt cellar. Never dip a dirty knife tip into a shared salt cellar. If everyone at the table has their own salt cellar for their individual use, one can either use the tip of their knife or may take a pinch of salt with their fingers. Yes, we said fingers!

Many establishments offer pepper via a large, ornate pepper grinder. The waiter will come around and ask if you would like some. Look them in the eye, and clearly and politely say either, "Yes, please." or "No, thank you." Most will grind until you say, "That is fine, thank you." So pay attention.

Applying this in the real world

Q. You said when given a choice, we should always pass to the right. What do I do when the person immediately to my left or two seats over asks for something. Do I still pass to the right and make them wait for the item?

A. You let common sense dictate and pass the item to the left so that it gets to them more quickly.

Q. I am sitting at a table of 10. When I do my job and start the breadbasket before anyone asks for it, shouldn't I get rewarded by taking a roll first before passing it to my right?

A. No, you shouldn't. Instead, say to the person on your left, "Before I pass the breadbasket to the right, would you like to take a roll?" Hold firmly onto the breadbasket so they cannot take it. When they are done, then take your own roll and pass the basket to the person on your right. This makes you look gracious and not gluttonous. This also works with the gravy boat, cream, and salad dressings—items that you cannot hold onto while the person on your immediate left uses it. Here you need to make sure you clearly signal that you are going to use the item as well so that they don't start it around the table the other way. "Before I pour my gravy, would you like some?" And if they do by chance forget to give it back to you, just wait for the item to make its way back. It will. Be patient. And if it stalls on the other side of the table, ask that it be passed to you.

28

Dessert and Finger Bowls

Dessert signals that you are getting to the end of the meal. As we discussed in Chapter 23, sometimes the table is set such that the dessert utensils are found at the top of the place setting. The spoon handle will be towards the right, while the fork handle is towards the left of the place setting. It is set this way so that when the diner moves the utensils down (to be next to the dessert plate), the handles will line up just like the fork and spoon of the earlier courses. Move the utensils down after your main course plate and utensils have been removed from the table. The wait-staff will then place your dessert plate in between the dessert fork and spoon.

At most formal dining occasions, the dessert course's presentation is a bit more elaborate. In these instances, wait-staff may carry out the dessert plate with a doily directly on the plate, underneath a finger bowl. The dessert fork and spoon will be on either side of the finger bowl on the dessert plate, instead of being found on the table. Again, it is your job to move the fork and spoon to their proper locations. Don't let the fancy finger bowl and doily throw you. Calmly lift both the doily and the finger bowl and place them to the upper left of your place setting, above your fork. The bowl and doily stay there, untouched. At this point, wait-staff will come out and serve you dessert on the now empty dessert plate. At the beginning of the dessert course, wait-staff may pour a glass a champagne which will be used for a toast. If they pour champagne, do not immediately take a sip–wait to see if a toast is coming. (More on this later, in Chapter 29.)

Now it's time to eat the dessert. If you are more comfortable using only one utensil, do that. Forks are generally used to eat cakes, while spoons are good for ice cream and creamy dishes such as tiramisu and the like. The goal is to look confident as you handle your utensils. If you would like to use both utensils, do the following: hold your fork, tines down, in your non-dominant hand, and use it to help anchor the food to the plate. At the same time, hold the spoon in your dominant hand and use it to deliver the food up to your mouth. Whether you use one or both utensils, when you are done eating, place both utensils in the 10:20 finished position with the fork tines down and the spoon bowl facing up. Coffee is sometimes served with the dessert course or may be served after the dessert course with small sweets and candies.

Now it is time to gracefully move the finger bowl (and the doily) from the upper left of the place setting and place it directly in front of you, where the dessert plate was when you were eating from it. Dip your finger tips for one hand (don't simulate washing your hands in a sink), bring that hand down to your lap, and dry the fingertips with your napkin there. Repeat with the other hand's fingertips.

When the host places their napkin on the table, they are signaling that the meal is done. Follow their lead and loosely gather the napkin and gently place it (do not refold it) on the table, either to the left of the place setting, or if the plate has been removed, where the plate was.

Applying this in the real world

Q. I have a dessert and I don't know what to do or how to eat it.

A. Take your time and watch the host. Follow their lead. If it turns out you don't like the dessert after taking a small "No, thank you" taste, it is fine not to finish. Just discretely move it around a bit on the plate so it looks as though you ate more than you did.

Q. I was at a fancy dinner where finger bowls were used but they were brought out after the dessert course has been eaten and our plates were taken away. Do I still need to put the finger bowl to the left?

A. There are instances when the finger bowl is brought out after dessert. You do not need to move the finger bowl or doily, just immediately repeat the steps above of gently dipping your fingertips and wiping with the napkin.

Cheers to Us:

TOASTING

As Catherine always says, *"If you don't make it special no one else will either."*

Toasts aren't just for weddings. Many hosts like to make their entertaining much more special by doing toasts. Champagne toasts are fun and festive. But toasts can be done with non-alcoholic beverages too. It is not advised to toast with water, as many are superstitious of that practice and believe it brings bad luck. If you ever find yourself with an empty glass at the beginning of a toast, go with the flow and raise it to "cheer" as well. Generally, "clinking" of glasses is reserved for more social occasions, but if your business colleagues like to do so, feel free to join in.

There are a few types of toasts. Whichever toast you are going to make, signal to the room that you are about to start by standing, slightly raising your glass to indicate you want to do a toast (but bring glass down while talking or your arm will feel like it is about to fall off). **Do not clink it with a utensil.** Let a few people know you are about to start a toast so they can help you quiet the room and direct attention your way.

The first type of toast is a "welcome toast" given by the host on the early side of an event. It is literally to welcome everyone to the occasion. Since this is a toast to everyone as opposed to a specific person or couple, everyone may take a sip.

The second type of toast is the "guest of honor" toast given by the host at the beginning of the dessert course. The host does this to make the guest of honor feel special with a heartfelt toast by standing and saying, "I'd like to propose a toast to [insert name]." This phrase is followed with a few short kind sentences about the guest of honor. The host concludes by saying, "so please join me in toasting [insert name]" and lifting their glass and taking a sip. The guest of honor does not take a sip—one doesn't drink a toast to oneself, just like one does not sing "Happy Birthday" to oneself.

The third type of toast is the "reciprocal toast" given by the guest of honor to thank the host for their hospitality. After a few short, heartfelt sentences, the guest of honor invites everyone to join in the toast by saying, "so please join me in toasting [insert host's name] for a lovely evening" as they lift their glass and take a sip. It is then the host's turn to refrain from drinking. Again, one does not drink a toast to oneself. Other guests are then free to propose a toast if the occasion calls for it. Let your judgment guide you.

If you want to give a toast, make sure you **commence**–stand if you are talking to a large group. Hold the glass down near your waist and chest area while you speak. Be **concise**. No one likes a long toast. The best ones are the shortest ones–no more than a minute or two. **Conclude**. This is when you lift your glass and take a sip while never looking inside the glass. You look over the rim at the people you are with. Our last rule is to be **kind**. Never be mean or embarrass someone with a toast.

Applying this in the real world

Q. I am close to the guest of honor. Is it ok for me to talk about something personal?

A. It really depends. Is it something that is so personal that you think the guest of honor may prefer to keep private? When in doubt, don't say it. Also, keep in mind that you should not refer to "inside jokes". While inside jokes and stories clearly demonstrate that you and the guest of honor have a warm and genuine relationship, it will make others feel excluded.

Q. You gave good advice on what *not* to say. But what *do* I say in a toast?

A. It takes a lot of effort to make a toast look effortless. Take some time to do some thinking and strive to make it heartfelt. It is perfectly appropriate to get some help and inspiration from quotes or poems or songs or real-life stories. Any toast said with a kind spirit and a warm heart will be a success, as long as it is concise.

Table Talk:

BODY LANGUAGE

At the beginning of the book, we discussed the importance of being mindful of your body language. This includes being mindful of your body's actions at the dinner table. If your body language is not good, people will find it unappealing to dine with you.

If at all possible, sit by entering the chair on its right side. When you are being seated at a large table, please wait for at least half the table to arrive before taking your seat. When you remain standing, it makes it easier to walk around and introduce yourself and shake hands when your table companions arrive as opposed to leaning over the table to try to shake hands.

It is important to sit up straight when dining. This does not mean ram-rod straight and uncomfortable. Rather it means sitting up straight enough so that you are not slouching or otherwise looking slovenly. You want to look like a confident and pleasant dining companion. Bring the food up to your mouth. Do not bring your mouth down to the food. Do not goof around with the chair–no tipping the chair back. It is juvenile to do so, and you could hurt yourself or others nearby, including wait-staff.

Your cellphone and other personal items (sunglasses, medicine, umbrella, etc.) do not belong on the table. When your cellphone is within eyeshot, it is a distraction. You are there face-to-face with someone and it is important to give them the undivided attention they deserve. If you are expecting an important call–from a doctor, your boss, your nanny or the like–let your dining companion know and keep the cellphone on your lap under your napkin, or in your pocket, so that you will know if it vibrates. When the call comes in, quietly excuse yourself to quickly take the call. Apologize upon your return.

Your elbows should be in–they belong close to your body. This is true even when you are cutting. Do not spread your elbows out while cutting because it doesn't look very attractive and it is likely to invade the personal space of those dining next to you. Elbows do not belong on the table throughout the meal.

Make sure you talk to the individuals on both sides of you. It is not nice to monopolize one person and neglect another. Please don't talk with a mouth full of food. Taking small bites enable you to talk without long pregnant pauses while you chew, and chew, and chew. Eat quietly–no smacking your lips or chewing loudly or with your mouth open. If your food is hot, do not blow on it. Patiently wait for it to cool.

Do not gesture wildly when you are holding utensils. Place your utensils down in the proper "resting" position discussed in Chapter 26 when you are drinking and when you are resting between bites.

Ask people to, "please pass" items that are not within easy reach. It is impolite to stretch across the table or reach across someone else.

Do not drink with a mouth full of food. If you do, some of your food may end up in your glass—very unappetizing for your dining companions.

Sometimes your water is served with a lemon or lime garnish. Don't drink from a glass with the garnish on the rim. Either remove it and put it on your bread plate, or other plate, or put it in your glass. If the garnish is served on a plate in the form of lemon or lime wedges, spear the pulp part with your fork or pick it up with your hands, squeeze the juice into your glass as you use the other hand as a shield to avoid spraying your companions with the juice. Again, drop the garnish into your glass or place the used wedge on a side plate–your choice.

Try to pace yourself when eating so that you don't eat faster than your dining companions. You don't want to finish too early. Likewise, you don't want to eat so slowly that everyone else is waiting for you to finish a course.

If you need to excuse yourself mid-meal, do not say, "I need to go to the bathroom". Instead, say, "Please excuse me." They can probably guess where you are headed, no need to broadcast it.

There is no reason for you to handle your plate. When you are done, do not push the plate back. Do not hand your plate over to the wait-staff, unless they are having a hard time reaching you and they ask for some assistance. Do not stack plates. While you may be trying to help the wait-staff, you may, in fact, be making it more difficult for them to clear the table.

Applying this in the real world

Q. I have heard it is okay to put your elbows on the table between courses, is this true?

A. While some think it is okay to put elbows on the table between courses, we recommend against it. When you do that, you may end up inadvertently slightly turning your back toward one of your dining companions. Keeping your elbows off the table also keeps you from slouching. You look better sitting up.

Q. I find it difficult to talk to people on each side of me. What do I do when they are talking to the person on their other side? I have no one to talk too!

A. Socializing is an important part of the dining ritual. When you are seated at a larger table and have people on both sides of you, make a conscious effort to talk to each person. It is not nice to neglect someone. You may want to alternate conversation partners with each new course. Or you may want to alternate after a story or two. You don't want to be a ping-pong, but you should make an effort to balance your time. If the person you turn your attention to is speaking to someone on their other side, you have a few options. You can try to join in that conversation if able. You can try to talk to the person across the table, or you can return to the person you were just talking to on the other side. If everyone is occupied, don't worry. Simply smile and take a bite or two and a sip of your drink while you wait for an opening.

I Didn't Order That!

Even though you are well on the way to dazzling dining etiquette, you need to be ready for the unexpected. There are times when awkward things happen at the dining table. The first thing to remember is: "**stay calm when things go wrong**." This is the ideal time to showcase your marvelous manners. It is easy to be well-mannered when things are going swimmingly. It takes much more thought and self-restraint to showcase marvelous manners when things don't go according to plan. This chapter will review a few good rules of thumb to keep you pleasant in the face of unpleasantness.

On the rare occasion, you may find a piece of gravel, hair, or a dead bug on your plate. You are mortified and disgusted. Who wouldn't be? What do you do?

If you are dining in someone's home, it is best not to make a scene. You do not want to embarrass the host. Use your knife or fork to isolate the offending object from the still edible part of the dish. Do not touch the offending object with your utensils. Instead, cut beyond the offending object, creating a wide perimeter to divide clearly that part of your meal you will not eat. If you are out at a restaurant, the goal is still not to make a scene. But you have an additional option to the example given above. You may also quietly signal for the waiter and discretely and politely explain that there is a foreign object on your plate and you would prefer a new dish. Others will notice that you have sent your food back. If asked, just say, "they are fixing the dish". You need not gross anyone else out by explaining there was a dead bug or a piece of hair on your plate. That is unappetizing to hear. Encourage your companions to "please continue eating, I will catch up shortly." Then engage in conversation.

The other time when it is appropriate to send food back is when it is not prepared properly. You ordered rare and your steak arrived well. You ordered "dressing on the side" and your salad arrives swimming in a vinaigrette. You may also send it back if the food is inedible, tasting spoiled and such. Those are all perfectly acceptable times to send food back. When you send food back it is important to be quick, discrete, and polite.

Alternatively, when is it unacceptable to send food back?

- Sending food back because you "just don't like it" despite that it was properly prepared.
- You ordered incorrectly. That is on you–not the restaurant.
- Unless wine is truly corked–do not send a glass or bottle of wine back simply because you don't like the taste.

Sometimes you are enjoying a bite of food only to discover you bit into grizzle. You simply cannot swallow it. What to do? Discretely remove the piece of grizzle from your mouth with your finger and thumb and return it to the edge of your plate and try to bury it under other food so no one is forced to see it while they eat their own food.

Sometimes you didn't order a sneeze, but you feel one coming on. What do you do? This scenario is exactly why you should always have a tissue or a handkerchief handy. If you don't have one and you feel a massive sneeze coming–one that requires a tissue–turn away from the table, into your shoulder and use your napkin as a shield. Once the sneeze has passed, excuse yourself from the table and take the napkin with you. Leave it in the bathroom and freshen up. Napkins should not be used as handkerchiefs but if it is the only thing available in an emergency, common sense should prevail–use it. Then ask for a fresh napkin upon returning to the table.

Sometimes you find yourself with a rude dining companion–one that treats wait-staff rudely, bothers those sitting at the next table with their loud, belligerent, and boisterous behavior, or treats you rudely during the meal. Hopefully, this will never happen to you, especially at a business meal, where people are supposed to be on their best, professional behavior. When you are out with a group of professionals for work and someone's behavior is rude, try to create as much physical space between you as possible. That can be hard to do if you are already seated. In that case, turn your complete attention to the others at the table and do not engage with that person. In this situation, others likely share your discomfort.

Applying this in the real world

Q. I have heard if I want to remove an unwanted item from my mouth that I should discard it onto my fork. Is that wrong?

A. You may certainly do that under one condition–that you can do it discretely. It is quite difficult to elegantly and discretely put a piece of grizzle or a bone back onto a fork. That is why we advise using your thumb and index finger and, in one swift motion, remove and discard items that way.

Q. What happens if I am at a business dinner, but it is only me and the person who turns out to be an offensive oaf and makes me feel very unsafe and uncomfortable?

A. If someone's behavior is extremely offensive to you and you are dining alone, feel free to calmly excuse yourself. This is when a little white lie is your friend. Simply offer a weak smile and say, "I so apologize but I am suddenly feeling quite ill. I must go. Again, my apologies." Then get up and leave–do not engage in a debate about whether or not you should leave. Stand up and leave. If it was a colleague's offensive behavior, talk to your boss. If it was your boss, talk to your HR coordinator. If it was a client, again, talk to your boss. Being a motivated and professional employee does not mean you must be subjected to unprofessional behavior that makes you feel unsafe or uncomfortable. This is a facts and circumstances situation and you need to quickly assess it and trust your gut.

Tea Time

"Tea is a cup of life." - Unknown

Instead of a business breakfast, lunch, or dinner, you may soon be invited to a business tea. It can be unnerving if you don't know what to do when. First things first, pinkies down. You don't properly engage in the gentle ritual of tea by putting on airs. To properly participate in this unquestionably social and civilized event, you must showcase your good manners through pleasant conversation and gracious behavior[28]. That means making everyone feel comfortable. Raising your pinkie is just snobby. The traditional time for tea is four o'clock in the afternoon with tea rooms normally serving between the hours of three and five o'clock. Whatever time you have a business afternoon tea, its ritual should illustrate to you the importance of etiquette in everyday life.

Once you learn proper tea etiquette, you will be comfortable and confident and can then focus on making others feel welcome. There are many types of tea service–high tea, afternoon tea, cream tea, light tea, and royal. We are going to review what is served at an **afternoon tea**. Tea sandwiches, scones, pastries, and cakes are served with the tea during this type of tea service.

After greeting your tea companion, take your seat. Wait for your host to place their napkin on their lap and then follow suit. The tea napkin is smaller than the normal formal lunch and dinner napkins. A tea napkin is 12 inches and to properly use it, open it fully under the table and place it on your lap.

All the traditional rules of dining etiquette apply when you are at a tea and there are a few additional rules about tea and the food served at a tea worth mentioning as well.

The host or another guest can pour tea from a common pot one cup at a time, wait-staff may pour your tea directly into your teacup, or you may receive an individual pot from which you pour and prepare your own tea. To avoid spills, do not fill the teacup up to the rim. Leave extra room.

If someone else pours your tea and asks you how you take it, simply state what you would like added or say that you take it "plain, please." Tea is often served with a choice of milk, sugar, lemon, or honey. While you may add what you like to your tea, remember that one does not usually add both milk and lemon (lemon makes the milk curdle), while sugar is added before lemon (because the lemon's acidity prevents the sugar from dissolving). Cream is never added to tea–it is quite heavy and will overwhelm the tea.

Once the desired ingredients are added to your teacup, quietly and gently stir them in with your teaspoon. The spoon never touches the side of the cup. No clanging noises, please! When you are done, lay the teaspoon on the teacup's saucer behind the cup. The spoon's handle should point in the same direction as your teacup's.

If the pot is filled with hot water and accompanied with a tea bag on the side, it is your job to add the tea bag into the pot of water. If there is loose-leaf tea inside your individual tea pot, you will be provided a tea strainer (a mini strainer with handles wide enough to rest on a teacup). Rest the tea strainer on the rim of your teacup and pour the tea into it. The strainer will catch the tea leaves, keeping them from ending up in your teacup. Remove the tea strainer from the teacup and return it to its resting bowl. Use it each time you want to pour tea (if you don't, your teacup will be filled with floating leaves). Fill your teacup only three-quarters of the way full to prevent spills, then add ingredients as noted above.

If you are served a teacup with a tea bag resting on the saucer, it is your job to prepare your cup of tea. Add the tea bag to the cup of water and patiently let it steep. Do not pull the tea bag string to quickly lift and lower the tea bag. You do not help it steep more quickly; you only look restless. Once it is done steeping (a few minutes time), gently remove the tea bag–one never drinks a cup of tea with a tea bag still inside. When removing the tea bag from your cup, do not wind the string around the bag to wring out all the tea. Right before you pull the tea bag out of the cup, quickly press it against the side of the cup with your spoon (so it isn't dripping wet). Then place it on a separate plate or saucer, ideally not the one under your cup.

Never grip the saucer between your thumb and index finger when trying to hold it. Instead, hold the saucer with a teacup on it by spreading your fingers as you cradle the saucer in your palm with your fingertips securing the rim. Your thumb assists. Your other hand handles the teacup. Put your index finger through the teacup handle, your middle finger right under the handle and your remaining fingers naturally rounded.

Your thumb grips the handle of the teacup for balance. Raise the cup to your lips, sit up straight and enjoy a cup of tea.

The saucer and teacup are partners. If you are seated without a table nearby, hold the saucer and teacup above your knees. If you are seated at a table, don't lift the saucer when taking a sip of tea, except if there is more than a foot between you and the table. Then it looks more elegant to lift the saucer as you take a sip of tea. Likewise, if you are standing, hold the saucer and teacup as a pair. Hold the saucer around your lower ribs and gently raise your teacup to your lips.

One usually sees a three-tiered stand at afternoon teas. Tea sandwiches (savories) are on the bottom, scones and cakes are on the middle, and, lastly, sweets, chocolates, small tarts, and desserts are on the top. Start eating from the bottom and work your way up, only taking your fair share. Just because you skip the savories does not mean you can double up on the scones. Teas are not all-you-can-eat buffets.

Tea sandwiches are finger foods and properly eaten without utensils. Enjoy!

There are multiple ways to properly eat **scones**. Even though you are at a business meal, we recommend eating scones with your fingers by breaking off small, individual pieces, one at a time. Jam and clotted cream may be added to each piece; spread the jam first then add a small bit of cream, if desired. If butter, jam, and honey are served instead, the butter goes on the scone first followed by either the jam or honey.

The table should have common bowls with accompanying serving spoons of each condiment. Use the communal serving spoon to place a spoonful of the desired condiment on your plate. Then use your individual knife to spread the condiments on each piece, again, one at a time. Repeat as desired.

You may also eat the scone by horizontally slicing it in half and eating a slice at a time. Starting with the bottom slice, use your knife to add one bite's worth of condiment. Take a bite. Place the scone back on your plate to add another bite's worth of condiment. Once you are done with the bottom slice repeat the process with the top slice. There is the option of spreading the condiment on the entire slice and then eating one bite at a time. While more efficient, it can get messy, so we do not recommend it at a business tea.

If you do not want to eat the scone with your fingers, you can use utensils. After slicing the scone horizontally in half and adding the desired condiments to your plate, you can then spread them on the entire slice (like you would a slice of toast), starting with the top slice. An easy way to remember to eat the *top* scone slice first is that some consider it "*over-the-top*" to eat scones with utensils. Use your fork and knife to cut and transport each piece to your mouth. You may use either the American or Continental style of eating. After you finish with the top scone slice, proceed to the bottom scone slice.

Cakes should be eaten with a fork. The tarts and other sweets on the top tier may be eaten with your fingers if they are not sticky or messy. This is a facts-and-circumstance situation. Otherwise, please use a utensil.

Applying this in the real world

Q. What do I do when I spill a bit of my tea onto my saucer? I don't want to drip on my clothes, but I don't want to stop sipping the tea.

A. The best way to avoid this is to make sure you don't overfill your cup and you don't stir too vigorously. But tea spills happen. Stay calm and politely request a paper napkin to soak it up. Once you are done, if there is a separate saucer or plate discard the napkin there. If no such saucer is provided, keep the napkin where it is and continue to sip your tea.

Q. I like to add lemon slices to my cup of tea. What do I do with it when I want a second cup of tea?

A. Lemon slices are added after the tea is poured. If you would like another cup of tea, remove the lemon slice with a lemon fork or other utensil to make room for a fresh slice. A separate plate should be provided for the discarded lemons. If one is not provided, politely request one.

33

You Have This Covered:

HOW TO BE A WELL-MANNERED HOST AT A BUSINESS MEAL

As you advance in your career, you will likely take business associates out to eat to further your relationship. You will be the host. There are responsibilities that come with being a host of a business meal. It takes effort to make a business meal look effortless. If you do it well, it serves as a proxy of you being a well-mannered, competent professional. If you don't handle it well, your dining companion may very well wonder what else you don't handle well. But not to worry; what follows is all you need to know to be a well-mannered host.

As the host, it is your responsibility to extend an invitation. A business meal is an opportunity to show the other person your appreciation as well as an opportunity to get to know someone a bit better away from a typical business setting. Don't forgo the first opportunity to show your sincerity of deepening your relationship by delegating this responsibility to your assistant. Your responsibility is to extend a detailed invitation–with a date, a time, and a location. Do not reach out to someone and ask, "when can you do lunch", or "where do you want to go" or "send me some dates that work for you". When you ask those questions, you shift the responsibilities of the host onto your guest. **Bad Form**.

Pick a restaurant that is within your price range so that you can easily cover the entire bill and one that is conveniently located for your guest. Make sure that it has an atmosphere appropriate for what you want your meal to accomplish. If you want to be able to speak freely without being overheard, pick a location that is quiet and has space between tables. If you want to be seen, choose a restaurant popular in your line of work or one that you know. If you are "a regular", wait-staff will go out of their way to ensure your experience is top-drawer.

Confirm your reservation with the restaurant and send a short reminder email to your guest the morning of or the afternoon before your scheduled get-together. Arrive at the restaurant early so that your guest isn't waiting for you. You may wait for your guest to arrive before you are seated. If you do this, you will greet your guest at the hostess station and allow them to immediately follow the host to the table. You will follow your guest. Alternatively, you can ask to be seated. When your guest arrives, the hostess will walk your guest to your table. As you see them approaching, stand and extend your hand. Asking to be seated as soon as you arrive gives you a few minutes to make sure everything is in order before your guest arrives. You see the table's location in the restaurant and can request a change if you don't like it. You meet the wait-staff and can establish that you are the host. This is helpful if you have time constraints or special requests that you don't want to highlight in front of your guest, such as, "I have a hard stop at 1:15 so would you please make sure bring me the bill by then."

While you wait for your guest, do not touch anything on the table– even the napkin. Do not order a drink. Tell the wait-staff, "Thank you," but you will order once your guest arrives. These actions enable your guest to see a pristine table. When your guest arrives, stand and greet them with a smile and an extended hand. Motion to the seat they should sit in, ideally it will be the "better" seat—the one with the better view of the restaurant or to your right. As the host, once you and your guest sit, immediately place your napkin on your lap.

If you have been to the restaurant before, it makes it easier for you to offer a few dish recommendations. If you want to send the signal that you are open to a multi-course meal, highlight a few appetizers as well as main dishes. Let your guest order first.

The days of the three-martini lunch are long past. You should forgo ordering alcohol first at lunch. If your guest wants a glass, use your judgment as to whether you join them. If you are celebrating a signed contract, a holiday, or a recent win, the mood will be festive, and you may want to join in. But whatever the occasion, never over-drink. Know your limits and stay well within them.

Do not immediately jump into shop talk. It is important to take advantage of the leisurely pace of a meal (certainly when compared to a normal conference call or meeting) to socialize and get to know each other. It is expected that there will be some socializing before getting to the agenda at hand. If you do want to discuss specific business, wait to bring it up until after the main course arrives.

When the bill arrives, immediately pick it up and provide your credit card or other payment. As the host, it is your responsibility to pay for the entire meal.

Applying this in the real world

Q. When I am seated at the table waiting for my guest, the wait-staff always asks me if I want a drink. May I order one?

A. Despite the fact that you should not order a drink while waiting for your guest, wait-staff ask the question. They are trying to provide good service. Tell the waiter that you are waiting for your guest and then will order something.

Q. I often take people to lunch, but the wait-staff always hands the check to the other person. It's awkward. What should I do?

A. Make sure you get to the restaurant first so that you can send the message that you are the host of the event. Ask to be seated at your table. Meet the wait-staff and indicate that you are the host. Let them know any specific requests that you have for the meal, including that you would like the check handed directly to you.

34

Thank You for the Kind Invitation:

How to be the Perfect Guest at a Business Meal

Likewise, as you advance in your career, you are likely to be invited out to breakfast, lunch, or dinner. As a guest, you have responsibilities too. Done well, you will convey you are confident and well-mannered and successfully expand your networking circle.

Upon receiving an invitation to lunch, promptly reply and put it on your calendar. RSVP. If you need to cancel for any reason, do so personally–that is not something you delegate to a subordinate. If the invitation was extended over phone, call the person to apologetically cancel. If the invitation was extended over email, send an email cancelling as soon as possible.

If you are invited to someone's home or to an event where you don't order from a menu, you mention food allergies when you accept the invitation. They need to know about food allergies as far in advance as possible and you need to take charge of your health. Safety first, people! Notice, we said "allergies"–not food "preferences". There is a difference. Keep preferences to yourself.

Prepare for the lunch by reading the morning trades so you are up on the latest industry happenings. At the same time, it is important to read the morning papers and other material so that you have something other than work to discuss. By doing this bit of prep, you can talk about more than just business. Arts, leisure, and travel topics help convey that you are well-rounded.

Arrive on time. Greet your host with a handshake, good posture, and a smile. Look confident to set the tone for a successful lunch. Be a positive dining companion and conversationalist so please no complaining about the taxi, the weather, the food, or gossiping.

At restaurants, you will enjoy plate service where your food is plated in the kitchen and served by wait-staff. Your food will be served from your left and cleared from your right by the wait-staff. You should not move the plate or stack them in an attempt to help things along. Drinks will be poured and removed on your right. This ensures that the wait-staff doesn't need to reach across you to pour drinks or take glasses.

Sometimes you will attend a charity, business, or other event where you are seated at a ten-top and wait-staff serves everyone the same meal. Wait-staff may serve you plated food or they may serve you from a common platter. They may transfer the food from the main platter to your dish themselves or they may signal to you to pick up the serving utensils from the platter and serve yourself. When you are done serving yourself (take only your fair share so everyone has enough), return the utensils faced down with the handles side-by-side on the edge of the platter so that the next diner may easily use them.

It is important to treat wait-staff well. Things will go wrong from time to time. When they do, it is important for you to stay calm and carry on. No one likes a complainer and treating others poorly makes your dining companions uncomfortable. That behavior does not reflect well on you or your organization. You can help the wait-staff by keeping the floor areas to the left and right of your seat clear for their use. Small purses should go under your napkin on your lap. Briefcases and larger bags should go right at your feet or under your chair so wait-staff doesn't trip. It is best not to bring those items when dining. If the restaurant allows you to check those items when you check your coat, consider doing so.

Sometimes you will attend a buffet event. In these instances, after the wait-staff brings your drinks to the table, you will approach the buffet table or stations full of food and serve yourself. Take only one plate at a time and start at the beginning of the buffet and wait your turn. Do not cut someone else in line because you "just want the salad". Demonstrate patience and consideration by following the rules and flow of the buffet line. Do not overload your plate. Use the serving utensils—never grab with just your hands. Do not mix up serving utensils by taking them with you to use elsewhere. Even though all the food courses are out at once, you should prepare a plate one course at a time. You may return to the buffet for the dessert course so there is no need to add a slice of cake or cookies to your plate on your first visit to the buffet. Wait to eat until you are seated. Do not eat while in line.

Follow the host's lead when it comes to the meal. Ask the host what they recommend eating. This gives them the opportunity to talk and signal to you how they want the meal to proceed. If they mention a great appetizer, know they are expecting you to order one. Order items that are not difficult to eat so you look elegant and graceful during the meal. Ordering items in the mid-price range is appropriate. Do not order the most expensive item on the menu—it shows bad judgment. It is okay not to order dessert, but if your host does, order a coffee or tea so you have something in front of you too. Wait for your host to place their napkin on their lap before you do so. Wait for the host to pick up their utensils before you do so.

Show your sincere appreciation for the gift of a meal and their time by thanking your host at the end of the meal and following up with a handwritten thank you note. (See Chapter 22).

Applying this in the real world

Q. My boss took out our team to congratulate us on a recent success. We went to a very expensive restaurant and I had a wonderful dish. I wasn't able to finish my meal, so I asked for a doggie-bag. I didn't want my boss' hospitality to go to waste. My colleagues laughed at me. Was I wrong?

A. Your colleagues should not have laughed at your faux pas, but one does not ask for a doggie-bag at a business meal.

Q. I only want to order the entrée, but my boss always orders an appetizer. What do I do?

A. You follow your boss's lead. Likewise, if your client orders an appetizer, you should do so also. By ordering a light appetizer as well, you are being considerate of your dining companion. No one likes to eat a course alone.

THANK YOU

Thank you for taking the time to read, *The Marvelous Millennial's Manual to Modern Manners*. We had a ball writing it and hope you enjoyed reading it and learned a thing or two. We only included the most concise and up-to-date material you need to advance in your career and have a happier life. While we hope you use this as a reference guide, you may be wondering, "how can I remember it all?" Well, here is a little tidbit we do to help us put our best polite, polished foot forward every work day—the following rundown of our five senses:

1. **Sight**: While we shouldn't judge a book by its cover, many do. I make sure that I look appropriate for my day such that my deportment and wardrobe will reinforce my personal brand. My appearance works for me and not against me.

2. **Sound**: I will not invade the auditory space of those around me. I will not needlessly use speakerphone in the office or on my mobile device. I will not make irritating noise with my body by typing loudly, eating loudly or snapping my gum. I will not otherwise disturb others working in an open-work environment.

3. **Smell:** My fragrance should not arrive before my body does. My fragrance (perfume, after-shave) is pleasant and gentle so as to not give offense. My breath is fresh. I don't have body odor.

4. **Taste**: I will only use sweet words; I will not let the bitter taste of caustic words pass my lips. I will take every opportunity to say, "please", "thank you", "I'm sorry", and "you're welcome". I will not behave in poor taste by gossiping or swearing. I will clearly and confidently introduce myself and others.

5. **Touch**: I strive to improve everyone's day I touch. I will respect the personal space of others by not touching their personal belongings, looking at their work product, or approaching them from behind. I will remember to stand and properly shake hands with others. I will act so kindness touches everyone I encounter.

Our five senses walk with us every day. Running through this list only takes a minute. If you do this, you will be well on your way to becoming the best version of yourself. Remember, you are not putting on airs or trying to become someone else but are acting in a way that shows you respect yourself and you respect others. We make choices every day and if we choose wisely—to be kind and to act with self-respect—we will reap all the rewards that flow from being well-mannered and will have no need to ever regret our behavior.

We would love to keep in touch! Please visit us at https://www.marvelouslywell-mannered.com/join-us to sign up to receive our monthly blog newsletter. If you fill out the form by providing your name, email address, and type "Dining Skills Checklist Please!" in the subject line, we will also email you our exclusive *Top Ten Dining Skills Checklist*! How marvelous!

Sincerely,
Catherine & Jessica

ABOUT THE AUTHORS

Catherine C. Wallace and Jessica W. Marventano make up the mother-daughter team behind Marvelously Well-Mannered and are civility, etiquette, modern manners, and social skills experts, having appeared on CBS, ABC and FOX morning shows in the DC metro area. They provide civility and business etiquette,  personal branding, and dining skills classes, including classes at the prestigious Capitol Hill Club for congressional offices and corporate and non-profit government affairs teams. Catherine has a background in teaching while Jessica has spent the past fourteen years running the Government Affairs office of a Fortune 500 company. Having both worked on Capitol Hill in various capacities, these ladies know Washington and know manners, etiquette, and social skills matter in business–and in life. They are also the co-creators of the award-winning children's manners, social skills, and etiquette board game, KINDNESS KINGOM. Both Catherine and Jessica were trained by the Protocol School of Washington in business etiquette and international protocol and were trained to teach children by the International School of Protocol. They also both reside in Arlington, VA.

ENDNOTES

1   Neil Howe and William Strauss, *Generations: The History of American's Future, 1584-2069* (New York: Quill, 1991).

2   Sam Tanenhaus, "Generation Nice," *New York Times* (New York, New York), August 2014.

3   Lee Rainie, "New Workers, New Workplaces; Digital 'Natives' Invade the Workplace", *Pew Research Center* (2006).

4   Lindsay Pollak, "It's About Time We Stop Shaming Millennials," TEDxStLouisWomen, November 15, 2016. https://www.lindseypollak.com.

5   William L. Patty and Louise S. Johnson, *Personality and Adjustment,* (1953) 277.

6   "Millennials are the largest generation in the U.S. labor force," Pew Research Center (April 11, 2018). http://www.pewresearch.org/fact-tank/2018/04/11/millennials-largest-generation-us-labor-force/

7   Lindsey Pollak, "3 things every employer needs to know about millennials," Lindsey Pollak (blog), June 1, 2014, https://www.lindseypollak.com/3-things-every-employer-needs-to-know-about-millennials/.

8   Lucinda Holdforth, *Why Manners Matter*, (New York: Amy Einhorn Books, 2009).

9   Peter Jones, "Top 7 Job Skills you'll need in 10 years if you don't want to be left behind.," *The Job Network* (2016).

10 Kate Davidson, "Employers Find "Soft Skills" Like Critical Thinking in Short Supply," *Wall Street Journal* (August 30, 2016).

11   Research by Harvard University, The Carnegie Foundation, and the Stanford Research Institute shows that 85 percent of one's professional success is connected to one's social skills.

12   A University of North Carolina at Chapel Hill's Kenan-Flagler Business School 1999 study found that more than 50 percent of people spend work time worrying about toxic colleague and 10 percent spend less time at work as a result.

13   A University of North Carolina at Chapel Hill's Kenan-Flagler Business School 1999 study found 45 percent of people think about finding a new job because of rudeness at work and 12 percent did change jobs.

14   Adam C. Uzialko, "Is A Hostile Workplace Making Your Employees Miserable?," *Business News Daily* (August 20, 2017), https://www.businessnewsdaily.com/10165-hostile-workplace-hazardous-conditions.html.

15   Adam Uzualko, "Is A Hostile Workplace Making Your Employees Miserable?," *Business News Daily* (August 20, 2017). Noting research by Rand Corporation, Harvard Medical School, and the University of California, Los Angeles that found that 1 in 5 workers faced hostile conditions—verbal abuse, threats, sexual harassment and bullying.

16   Study by Dr. Kenneth Hansraj, chief of spine surgery at New York Spine Surgery and Rehabilitation Medicine.

17   Patricia Rossi, *Everyday Etiquette*, (New York: St. Martin's Press, 2011).

18   Nancy Etcoff, "Cosmetics as a Feature of the Extended Human Phenotype: Modulation of the Perception of Biologically Important Facial Signals," *PLOS* (October 2011), https://doi.org/10.1371/journal.pone.0025656.

19   Letitia Baldrige, *Taste,* (New York: St. Martin's Press, 2007) 2. Professor P.M. Forni is the author of two excellent books on

civility we highly recommend: *Choosing Civility* (St. Martin's Press 2002) and *The Civility Solution* (St. Martin's 2008).

20 Peggy Noonan, "If Adults Won't Grow Up, Nobody Will" From Facebook to Harvey Weinstein, America's scandals amount to a giant crisis of maturity, (*The Wall Street Journal*, April 5, 2018).

21 Carrie Kerpen, "Yes, It Matters What You Wear to Work," (Forbes.com February 28, 2017).

22 Judith Martin, *Miss Manners' Guide to Excruciatingly Correct Behavior*, (New York: W.W. Norton & Company, 2005) 26.

23 P.M. Forni, *Choosing Civility*, (New York: St. Martin's Griffin, 2002) 21-24.

24 P.M. Forni, *Choosing Civility*, (New York: St. Martin's Griffin, 2002).

25 Sue Shellenbarger, "The Smartest Ways to Network at a Party," *The Wall Street Journal* (September 14, 2015)

26 Helena Tate, "You Can Speak to Anyone, Anywhere ....," MFS eCourse Week 3 (2010).

27 Remarks by Federal Communications Commission Chairman Ajit Pai before The Media Institute (November 29, 2017) https://www.fcc.gov/document/chairman-pai-remarks-media-institute.

28 Dorothea Johnson and Bruce Richardson, Tea & Etiquette, Taking Tea for Business and Pleasure, (Benjamin Press, 2009). This is an excellent book that provides a history of tea, a complete review of all types of tea service, and in-depth accompanying etiquette. We encourage you to read it in its entirety.